FUNDAMENTALS OF
English
Grammar

FOURTH EDITION

WORKBOOK

Volume B

Betty S. Azar
Rachel Spack Koch
Stacy A. Hagen

Fundamentals of English Grammar, Fourth Edition
Workbook, Volume B

Azar Associates: Shelley Hartle, Editor, and Sue Van Etten, Manager

Pearson Education, 10 Bank Street, White Plains, NY 10606

Staff credits: The people who made up the *Fundamentals of English Grammar, Fourth Edition, Workbook*
   team, representing editorial, production, design, and manufacturing, are, Diane Cipollone, Dave Dickey,
   Christine Edmonds, Ann France, and Amy McCormick.

Text composition: S4Carlisle Publishing Services
Text font: 10.5/12 Plantin

Illustrations:
Don Martinetti: 133, 142, 143 (top), 144, 148, 149, 162, 173 (bottom), 179, 182, 184, 199, 202, 203, 207, 208,
214, 222, 223, 229, 240, 244, 245, 249, 250
Chris Pavely: 143 (bottom), 160, 173 (top), 192, 252

Printed in the United States of America

ISBN 10: 0-13-707490-5
ISBN 13: 978-0-13-707490-7

1 2 3 4 5 6 7 8 9 10—V042—16 15 14 13 12 11

Contents

Chapter 13   GERUNDS AND INFINITIVES

Chapter 14   NOUN CLAUSES

SPECIAL WORKBOOK SECTION

Appendix 1   PHRASAL VERBS

Appendix 2   PREPOSITION COMBINATIONS

Preface

The *Fundamentals of English Grammar Workbook* is a place for lower-intermediate and intermediate students to explore and practice English grammar on their own. It is a place where they can test and fine-tune their understanding of English structures and improve their ability to use English meaningfully and correctly. All of the exercises have been designed for independent study, but this book is also a resource for teachers who need exercise material for additional classwork, homework, testing, or individualized instruction.

The *Workbook* is keyed to the explanatory grammar charts found in *Fundamentals of English Grammar, Fourth Edition*, a classroom teaching text for English language learners, and in the accompanying *Chartbook*, a reference grammar with no exercises.

The answers to the practices can be found in the *Answer Key* in the back of the *Workbook*. Its pages are perforated so that they can be detached to make a separate booklet. However, if teachers want to use the *Workbook* as a classroom teaching text, the *Answer Key* can be removed at the beginning of the term.

Two special Workbook sections called *Phrasal Verbs* and *Preposition Combinations*, not available in the main text, are included in the Appendices. These sections provide reference charts and a variety of exercises for independent practice.

Chapter 8
Connecting Ideas

▶ **Practice 1. Connecting ideas with *and*.** (Chart 8-1)
<u>Underline</u> the words that are connected with *and*. Label these words as nouns, verbs, or adjectives.

                            noun + *noun* + *noun*
1. My kitchen has a new <u>sink</u>, <u>refrigerator</u>, and <u>oven</u>.

                    adjective + *adjective*
2. Danny is a <u>bright</u> and <u>happy</u> child.

           verb + *verb*
3. I picked up the telephone and dialed Steve's number.

4. I have a computer, a printer, and a scanner in my home office.

5. The cook washed the vegetables and put them in boiling water.

6. My feet were cold and wet.

7. Anita is responsible, considerate, and trustworthy.

8. The three largest land animals are the elephant, the rhinoceros, and the hippopotamus.

9. A hippopotamus rests in water during the day and feeds on land at night.

► **Practice 2. Punctuating sentences.** (Chart 8-1)
Each of these sentences contains two independent clauses. Find the subject "S" and verb "V" of each clause. Add a comma or a period. Capitalize as necessary.

     S V   S V
1. Birds fly, and fish swim.

     S V   S V
              F
2. Birds fly. fish swim.

3. Dogs bark lions roar.

4. Dogs bark and lions roar.

5. A week has seven days a year has 365 days.

6. A week has seven days and a year has 365 days.

7. Ahmed raised his hand and the teacher pointed at him.

8. Ahmed raised his hand the teacher pointed at him.

► **Practice 3. Punctuating items connected with *and*.** (Chart 8-1)
Add commas where necessary.

1. I opened the door and walked into the room. (No change.)
2. I opened the door, walked into the room, and sat down at my desk.
3. Their flag is green and black.
4. Their flag is green black and yellow.
5. Tom ate a sandwich and drank a glass of juice.
6. Tom made a sandwich poured a glass of juice and sat down to eat his lunch.
7. Ms. Parker is intelligent friendly and kind.
8. Mr. Parker is grouchy and unhappy.
9. Did you bring copies of the annual report for Sue Dan Joe and Mary?
10. I always read the newspaper online and listen to the news on the radio in the morning.
11. Can you watch television listen to the radio and read the newspaper at the same time?

► **Practice 4. Punctuating sentences.** (Chart 8-1)
Write "C" if the punctuation is correct and "I" for incorrect. Make the necessary corrections.

1. _____ Amy jogged along the road I rode my bicycle.
2. _____ Amy stopped after 20 minutes. I continued on for an hour.
3. _____ Trained dogs can lie down and perform other tricks on command.
4. _____ My mother trained our dog to get the newspaper, my father trained it to bark at strangers.
5. _____ The river rose, it flooded the towns in the valley.
6. _____ The river and streams rose. They flooded the towns and farms in the valley.

7. _____ Astrology is the study of the stars, planets and their effect on our lives.

8. _____ Sharon reads her horoscope every day. She believes her life is shaped by the positions of the stars and planets.

9. _____ Sharon's children don't believe in astrology, they dismiss the information she gives them.

▶ **Practice 5. Connecting ideas with *and*.** (Chart 8-1)

Part I. Read the passage.

Very Old Twins

Kin Narita and Gin Kanie were twin sisters from Japan. They were born in 1892. Their family name was Yano. Their first names are names of valuable metals: silver and gold. Kin means silver and Gin means gold.

They were 99 years old when the mayor of Nagoya, their hometown, visited them. He visited them on a national holiday—Respect for the Aged Day. In Japan, many people live a long time and receive a lot of respect when they are old. The mayor congratulated the twins on their long and healthy lives.

After the mayor's visit, the twins became famous and popular. They appeared on television game shows and in advertisements. People liked their wide smiles and their lively interest in the world. They laughed and smiled a lot. They said they stayed healthy because they had a simple lifestyle, walked everywhere, and enjoyed people, especially each other.

Kin had 11 children, and Gin had five children. They had many grandchildren and great-grandchildren. Kin died in January, 2000, at the age of 107, and Gin died in February, 2001, at the age of 108.

Part II. Each statement is incorrect. Make true statements. Write the correct punctuation.

1. The twins' first names mean health and happiness.

   _____ *The twins' first names mean silver and gold.* _____

2. In Japan, many people don't live a long time, and they don't receive respect when they are old.

   _____

   _____

3. The twins were young and sick.

   _____

4. The twins rarely laughed and smiled.

   _____

5. The twins never had a simple lifestyle and always drove everywhere.

   _____

6. They didn't enjoy people and they didn't enjoy each other.

   _____

7. Kin and Gin didn't have any children or grandchildren.

   _____

8. When they died Kin and Gin were together.

   _____

► **Practice 6. Using *and, but,* and *or.*** (Chart 8-2)
Add commas where necessary.

1. I talked to Amy for a long time, but she didn't listen.

2. I talked to Martin for a long time and asked him many questions. (No change.)

3. Please call Jane or Ted.

4. Please call Jane and Ted.

5. Please call Jane Ted or Anna.

6. Please call Jane Ted and Anna.

7. Did you call Kim or Luis?

8. I didn't call Leo Sarah or Hugo.

9. I waved at my friend but she didn't see me.

10. I waved at my friend and she waved back.

► **Practice 7. Connecting ideas with *so.*** (Chart 8-3)
Complete each sentence with a correct phrase from the list.

a. everybody laughed	e. she doesn't walk yet
b. I hung up	f. she walks and runs everywhere
c. I left a message	g. the grass got brown and dry
d. nobody laughed	h. the grass was green and bright

1. The joke was very funny, so _____.

2. The joke wasn't funny, so _____.

3. It didn't rain all summer, so _____.

4. It rained a lot this summer, so _____.

5. Our baby is only three months old, so _____.

6. Our baby is two years old, so _____.

7. The phone rang ten times, and nobody answered, so _____.

8. The phone rang three times, and a machine answered, so _____.

► **Practice 8. Using *and, but, or,* and *so.*** (Charts 8-1 → 8-3)
Choose the correct completion.

1. I was tired, _____ I went to bed.
    a. but   b. or   c. so

2. I sat down on the couch _____ opened the newspaper.
    a. but   b. and   c. so

3. The students were on time, _____ the teacher was late.
    a. but   b. or   c. so

4. I would like one pet. I'd like to have a bird _____ a cat.
    a. but   b. and   c. or

5. Our children are happy _____ healthy.
   a. but   b. and   c. or

6. I wanted a cup of tea, _____ I boiled some water.
   a. but   b. and   c. so

7. The phone rang, _____ I didn't answer it.
   a. but   b. and   c. so

8. You can have an apple _____ an orange. Choose one.
   a. but   b. and   c. or

▶ **Practice 9. Using *and*, *but*, *or*, and *so*.** (Charts 8-1 → 8-3)
Write "C" if the punctuation is correct and "I" for incorrect. Make the necessary corrections.

1. _____ I washed and dried the dishes.

2. _____ I washed the dishes, and my son dried them.

3. _____ Victor offered me an apple or a peach.

4. _____ I bought some apples peaches and bananas.

5. _____ I was hungry so I ate an apple.

6. _____ Carlos was hungry and ate two apples.

7. _____ My sister is generous and kind-hearted.

8. _____ My daughter is affectionate shy independent and smart.

▶ **Practice 10. Using *and*, *but*, *or*, and *so*.** (Charts 8-1 → 8-3)
Add periods, commas, and capital letters as necessary. Don't change any of the words or the order of the words.

1. James has a cold. *H* he needs to rest and drink plenty of fluids, so he should go to bed and drink water fruit juices or soda pop he needs to sleep a lot so he shouldn't drink fluids with caffeine, such as tea or coffee.

2. The normal pulse for an adult is between 60 and 80 beats per minute but exercise nervousness excitement and a fever will all make a pulse beat faster the normal pulse for a child is around 80 to 90.

3. Edward Fox was a park ranger for 35 years during that time, he was hit by lightning eight times the lightning never killed him but it severely burned his skin and damaged his hearing.

▶ **Practice 11. Using *and*, *but*, *or*, and *so*.** (Chart 8-1 → 8-3)
Add commas where necessary. Some sentences need no commas.

An English School for Gina

Gina wants a job as an air traffic controller. Every air traffic controller worldwide uses English so it is important for her to become fluent in the language. She has decided to take some intensive English courses at a private language institute but she isn't sure which one to attend. There are many schools available and they offer many different kinds of classes. She has also heard of air traffic control schools that include English as part of their coursework but she needs to have a fairly high level of English to attend. She has to decide soon or the classes will be full. She's planning to visit her top three choices this summer and decide on the best one for her.

▶ **Practice 12. Using auxiliary verbs after *but*.** (Chart 8-4)
Complete each sentence with the correct auxiliary verb.

1. Dan didn't study for the test, but Amy _____*did*_____.

2. Alice doesn't come to class every day, but Julie _____.

3. Jack went to the movie last night, but I _____.

4. I don't live in the dorm, but Rob and Jim _____.

5. My roommate was at home last night, but I _____.

6. Mr. Wong isn't here today, but Miss Choki _____.

7. Susan won't be at the meeting tonight, but I _____.

8. Susan isn't going to go to the meeting tonight, but I _____.

9. I'll be there, but she _____.

10. I haven't finished my work yet, but Erica _____.

11. My son enjoys monster movies, but I _____.

12. I enjoy romantic comedies, but my son _____.

▶ **Practice 13. Using auxiliary verbs after *and*.** (Chart 8-5)
Complete each sentence with the correct auxiliary verb.

1. Rob lives in the dorm, and Jim _____ too.

2. I don't live in the dorm, and Carol _____ either.

3. Ted isn't here today, and Linda _____ either.

4. The teacher is listening to the CD, and the students _____ too.

5. I'll be there, and Mike _____ too.

6. I can speak French, and my wife _____ too.

7. Jane would like a cup of coffee, and I _____ too.

8. I like rock music, and my roommate _____ too.

9. Paul can't speak Spanish, and Larry _____ either.

10. I am exhausted from the long trip, and my mother _____ too.

11. I have a dimple in my chin, and my brother _____ too.

12. I visited the museum yesterday, and my friend _____ too.

▶ **Practice 14. Using *and* + *too, so, either, neither*.** (Chart 8-5)
Complete the sentences by using the word in *italics* and an appropriate auxiliary.

1. *Tom*   Jack has a mustache, and so _____*does Tom*_____.

   Jack has a mustache, and _____*Tom does*_____ too.

2. *Brian*   Alex doesn't have a mustache, and neither _____.

   Alex doesn't have a mustache, and _____ either.

3. *I*   Mary was at home last night, and so _____.

   Mary was at home last night, and _____ too.

4. *Jean*   I went to a movie last night, and so _____.

   I went to a movie last night, and _____ too.

5. *Jason* I didn't study last night, and neither _____.

I didn't study last night, and _____ either.

6. *Rick* Jim can't speak Arabic, and neither _____.

Jim can't speak Arabic, and _____ either.

7. *Laura* I like to go to science-fiction movies, and so _____.

I like to go to science-fiction movies, and _____ too.

8. *Alice* I don't like horror movies, and neither _____.

I don't like horror movies, and _____ either.

▶ **Practice 15. Using *too, so, either,* or *neither* after *and*.** (Chart 8-5)

Part I. Complete the sentences with an auxiliary + *too* or *either*.

1. I can't sew, and my roommate _____*can't either*_____.

2. I don't like salty food, and my wife _____.

3. Yesterday, Rosa Gomez came to class late and Mr. Nazari _____.

4. Andy knew the answer to the question, and Tina _____.

5. I couldn't understand the substitute teacher, and Yoko _____.

6. I'd rather stay home this evening, and my husband _____.

Part II. Complete the sentences with an auxiliary + *so* or *neither*.

7. Pasta is a famous Italian dish, and _____*so is*_____ pizza.

8. I didn't go to the bank, and _____ my husband.

9. I'm not a native speaker of English, and _____ Mr. Chu.

10. I've never seen a monkey in the wild, and _____ my children.

11. When we heard the hurricane warning, I nailed boards over my windows, and _____ all of my neighbors.

12. My brother and I are taking the same chemistry course. It is difficult, but I like it and _____ he.

▶ **Practice 16. Auxiliary verbs after *but* and *and*.** (Charts 8-4 and 8-5)
A woman is talking about her housemate, Hanna. Choose the correct completion from Column B.

Column A

1. I like cooking, and __*h*__.

2. I don't like housework, and Hanna ____.

3. I like gardening, and she ____.

4. I don't like snakes in our garden, and ____.

5. She likes to go jogging after work, and ____.

6. She doesn't like to play golf, and I ____.

7. She likes to watch old movies, and I ____.

8. She doesn't like to sleep late on weekends, and ____

Column B

a. do too

b. does too

c. doesn't either

d. don't either

e. neither do I

f. neither does she

g. so do I

h. so does Hanna

► **Practice 17. Adverb clauses with *because*.** (Chart 8-6)
Add periods, commas, and capital letters as necessary.

1. Because his coffee was cold, Jack didn't finish it. ~~he~~ *H* he left it on the table and walked away.

2. I opened the window because the room was hot a nice breeze came in.

3. Because the weather was bad we canceled our trip into the city we stayed home and watched TV.

4. Debbie loves gymnastics because she hopes to be on an Olympic team she practices hard every day.

5. Francisco is very good in math because several colleges want him to attend they are offering him full scholarships.

► **Practice 18. Adverb clauses with *because*.** (Chart 8-6)
Read each pair of phrases and circle the one that gives the reason (explains "why"). Then check the correct sentence.

1. (lose weight,) go on a diet

   ✓ Eric went on a diet because he wanted to lose weight.

   _____ Because Eric went on a diet, he wanted to lose weight.

2. didn't have money, couldn't buy food

   _____ The family couldn't buy food because they didn't have money.

   _____ Because the family couldn't buy food, they didn't have money.

3. be very busy, have several children

   _____ Because our neighbors are very busy, they have several children.

   _____ Our neighbors are very busy because they have several children.

4. go to bed, be tired

   _____ I am tired because I am going to bed.

   _____ Because I am tired, I am going to bed.

5. be in great shape, exercise every day

   _____ Because Susan exercises every day, she is in great shape.

   _____ Susan exercises every day because she is in great shape.

6. have a high fever, go to the doctor

   _____ Because Jennifer has a high fever, she is going to the doctor.

   _____ Jennifer has a high fever because she is going to the doctor.

► **Practice 19. Adverb clauses with *so* or *because*.** (Charts 8-3 and 8-6)
Complete the sentences with *so* or *because*. Add commas where appropriate. Capitalize as necessary.

1. a. He was hungry _, so_ he ate a sandwich.

   b. _____ *Because* _____ he was hungry, he ate a sandwich.

   c. He ate a sandwich _____ he was hungry.

2. a. _____ my sister was tired she went to bed.

   b. My sister went to bed _____ she was tired.

   c. My sister was tired _____ she went to bed.

3. a. Schoolchildren can usually identify Italy easily on a world map _____ it is shaped like a boot.

   b. _____ Italy has the distinctive shape of a boot schoolchildren can usually identify it easily.

   c. Italy has the distinctive shape of a boot _____ schoolchildren can usually identify it easily on a map.

▶ **Practice 20. Adverb clauses with *even though* and *although*.** (Chart 8-7)
Complete each sentence with the correct form of the verb in *italics*. Some verbs will be negative.

1. Even though I (*like*) _____*like*_____ fish, I don't eat it much.

2. Even though I (*like*) _____*don't like*_____ vegetables, I eat them every day.

3. Although my hairdresser (*be*) _____ expensive, I go to her once a week.

4. Even though the basketball game was over, the fans (*stay*) _____ in their seats cheering.

5. Although my clothes were wet from the rain, I (*change*) _____ them.

6. Even though Po studied for weeks, he (*pass*) _____ his exams.

7. Even though the soup was salty, everyone (*eat*) _____ it.

8. Although the roads (*be*) _____ icy, no one got in an accident.

▶ **Practice 21. Using *because* and *even though*.** (Charts 8-6 and 8-7)
Choose the correct completion.

1. Even though I was hungry, I _____ a lot at dinner.
   a. ate   b. didn't eat

2. Because I was hungry, I _____ a lot at dinner.
   a. ate   b. didn't eat

3. Because I was cold, I _____ my coat.
   a. put on   b. didn't put on

4. Even though I was cold, I _____ my coat.
   a. put on   b. didn't put on

5. Even though Mike _____ sleepy, he stayed up to watch the end of the game on TV.
   a. was   b. wasn't

6. Because Linda _____ sleepy, she went to bed.
   a. was   b. wasn't

7. Because Kate ran too slowly, she _____ the race.
   a. won   b. didn't win

8. Even though Jessica ran fast, she _____ the race.
   a. won   b. didn't win

▶ **Practice 22. Adverb clauses with *because* and *even though*.**
(Charts 8-6 and 8-7)
Complete the sentences with *even though* or *because*.

1. Yuko went to a dentist ____*because*____ she had a toothache.

2. Colette didn't go to a dentist _____ she had a toothache.

3. Jennifer went to a dentist _____ she didn't have a toothache. She just
   wanted a checkup.

4. Louie didn't iron his shirt _____ it was wrinkled.

5. Eric ironed his shirt _____ it was wrinkled.

6. _____ Dan is fairly tall, he can't reach the ceiling.

7. _____ Matt is very tall, he can reach the ceiling.

8. _____ Tim is shorter than Matt, he can't reach the ceiling.

9. _____ Nick isn't tall, he can reach the ceiling by standing on a chair.

DAN   MATT   TIM   NICK

▶ **Practice 23. Adverb clauses with *because* and *although*.** (Charts 8-6 and 8-7)
Complete the passage with *because* or *although*.

Pill Bottles with Child-Proof Caps

It's difficult to open some pill bottles _____ they have child-proof caps. In
                                                                                1
recent years, pill manufacturers have been making this type of bottle _____
                                                                                          2
they don't want children to open the bottles and eat the pills. The pills inside the bottle are often

attractive, and _____ they look like candy, they are not candy.
                                                              3

Last week there was a story on the news about a lucky baby. The baby found an open bottle of

aspirin tablets. _____ the pills looked just like candy, he started to eat them.
                                                          4
When his mother walked into the room, she saw her baby and the open bottle.

_____ she was frightened, she acted calmly. She immediately took the baby to
5

the emergency room at the nearby hospital. There the doctors realized that

_____ the baby had eaten pills for adults, he needed only minor treatment.
6

The mother saved her baby _____ she had acted quickly.
7

▶ **Practice 24. Using *even though/although* and *because*.** (Charts 8-6 and 8-7)
Choose the best completion.

1. I gave him the money because __c__.
    a. I didn't want to
    b. he had a lot of money
    c. I owed it to him

2. Although _____, the hungry man ate every bit of it.
    a. the bread was old and stale
    b. the cheese tasted good to him
    c. an apple is both nutritious and delicious

3. The nurse didn't bring Mr. Hill a glass of water even though _____.
    a. she was very busy
    b. she forgot
    c. he asked her three times

4. When she heard the loud crash, Marge ran outside in the snow although _____.
    a. her mother ran out with her
    b. she wasn't wearing any shoes
    c. she ran as fast as she could

5. Even though his shoes were wet and muddy, Brian _____.
    a. took them off at the front door
    b. walked right into the house and across the carpet
    c. wore wool socks

6. Alex boarded the bus in front of his hotel. He was on his way to the art museum. Because he ____, he asked the bus driver to tell him where to get off.
   a. was late for work and didn't want his boss to get mad
   b. was carrying a heavy suitcase
   c. was a tourist and didn't know the city streets very well

7. Although ____, Eric got on the plane.
   a. he is married
   b. he is afraid of flying
   c. the flight attendant welcomed him aboard

8. When I attended my first business conference out of town, I felt very uncomfortable during the social events because ____.
   a. we were all having a good time
   b. I didn't know anyone there
   c. I am very knowledgeable in my field

9. Everyone listened carefully to what the speaker was saying even though ____.
   a. they had printed copies of the speech in their hands
   b. she spoke loudly and clearly
   c. the speech was very interesting

10. Talil works in the city, but once a month he visits his mother, who lives in the country. He has to rent a car for these trips because ____.
    a. it is expensive
    b. he doesn't have a driver's license
    c. he doesn't own a car

▶ **Practice 25. Editing.** (Chapter 8)
Correct the errors.

1. I don't drink coffee, and my roommate ~~isn't~~ *doesn't* either.

2. The flight was overbooked, I had to fly on another airline.

3. Many people use computers for email the Internet and word processing.

4. Even my father works two jobs, he always has time to play soccer or baseball on weekends with his family.

5. I saw a bad accident and my sister too.

6. Oscar always pays his bills on time but his brother wasn't.

7. Because my mother is afraid of heights, I took her up to the observation deck at the top of the building.

8. Janey doesn't like to get up early and either Joe.

9. My mother and my father. They immigrated to this country 30 years ago.

10. Even though Maya is very intelligent, her parents want to put her in an advanced program at school.

▶ Practice 26. Word search puzzle. (Chapter 8)

Circle the connecting words from Chapter 8 in the puzzle. The words may be horizontal, vertical, or diagonal. The first letter of each word is highlighted in gray.

T	B	M	R	L	R	**B**		**A**
O	M	P	E	E	U	**B**		L
A	O	M	H	T	J	E		T
W	N	**T**	T	K	T	C		H
R	I	D	I	P	K	A		O
E	J	T	E	F	B	U		U
M	R	**O**	**N**	T	W	S		G
T	B	V	**S**	O	J	E		H

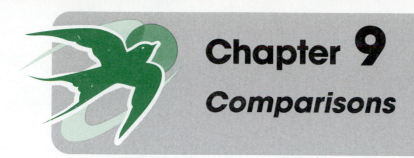

Chapter 9
Comparisons

▶ **Practice 1. As . . . as.** (Chart 9-1)
Make comparisons using **as . . . as.**

1. Rita is very busy. Jason is very busy.

   → Rita is _____(just) as busy as Jason (is)_____.

2. Rita is not very busy at all. Jason is very, very busy.

   → Rita isn't _____(nearly) as busy as Jason (is)_____.

3. I was tired. Susan was very tired.

   → I wasn't _____.

4. Adam wasn't tired at all. Susan was very tired.

   → Adam wasn't _____.

5. Anne is lazy. Her sister Amanda is equally lazy.

   → Anne is _____.

6. Their brother Alan is extremely lazy.

   → Anne and Amanda are lazy, but they are not _____.

▶ **Practice 2. As . . . as.** (Chart 9-1)
Make comparisons using **as . . . as** and the adjective in parentheses. Use **not** as necessary.

1. Adults have more strength than children. (*strong*)

   → Children _____aren't as strong as_____ adults.

2. Tom and Jerry are the same height. (*tall*)

   → Tom _____ Jerry.

3. Dr. Green has a little money. Dr. Brown has a lot of money. (*wealthy*)

   → Dr. Green _____ Dr. Brown.

4. City air is often polluted. Country air is often fresh and clear. (*polluted*)

   → Country air _____ city air.

5. Paula studies a little bit. Jack studies a lot. (*studious*)

   → Paula _____ Jack.

6. Math courses are easy for me, but language courses aren't. (*difficult*)

   → Math courses _____ language courses for me.

▶ **Practice 3. As . . . as.** (Chart 9-1)
Part I. Complete the sentences with one of the following:
- just as . . . as
- almost as . . . as / not quite as . . . as
- not nearly as . . . as

A   B   C   D

1. Building B is _____*not nearly as*_____ high as Building D.

2. Building A is _____ high as Building B.

3. Building C is _____ high as Building D.

4. Building A is _____ high as Building C.

Part II. Compare the arrival times. Meeting time: 9:00 A.M.

Arrival times

David 9:01 A.M.

Julia 9:14 A.M.

Laura 9:15 A.M.

Paul 9:15 A.M.

James 9:25 A.M.

5. Paul was _____*just as*_____ late as Laura.

6. David was _____ late as James.

7. Julia was _____ late as Laura and Paul.

8. Julia was _____ late as James.

Part III. Compare world temperatures.

Bangkok	92°F / 33°C
Cairo	85°F / 30°C
Madrid	90°F / 32°C
Moscow	68°F / 20°C
Tokyo	85°F / 30°C

9. Tokyo is _____ hot as Cairo.

10. Moscow is _____ hot as Bangkok.

11. Madrid is _____ hot as Bangkok.

Part IV. Compare world temperatures today and yesterday.

	Yesterday	*Today*
Bangkok	95°F / 35°C	92°F / 33°C
Cairo	95°F / 35°C	85°F / 30°C
Madrid	90°F / 32°C	90°F / 32°C
Moscow	70°F / 21°C	68°F / 20°C
Tokyo	81°F / 27°C	85°F / 30°C

12. Cairo was _____ hot as Bangkok yesterday.

13. It's _____ warm in Moscow today as yesterday.

14. Madrid is _____ hot today as yesterday.

15. It was _____ hot in Tokyo yesterday as in Bangkok.

16. It's _____ hot in Bangkok today as yesterday.

▶ **Practice 4. As . . . as.** (Chart 9-1)

Part I. Complete each expression with the correct phrase.

as a bat	as a mouse	as a pillow
as a bird	as a picture	✓ as snow
as a bone	as pie	as a wink
as ice		

bat

1. very white: as white ___*as snow*___.

2. very cold: as cold _____.

3. very pretty: as pretty _____.

4. can't see anything: as blind _____.

5. very dry: as dry _____.

6. very soft: as soft _____.

7. very quick: as quick _____.

8. very quiet: as quiet _____.

9. very free: as free _____.

10. very easy: as easy _____.

wink

pie

Part II. Complete the sentences with the given adjectives and the phrases from Part I.

blind	dry	free	quick	soft
✓cold	easy	pretty	quiet	white

11. Brrrr! Come inside. Your hands are freezing. They are as _____cold as ice_____.

12. I'm just running down to the corner store. I'll be back in a few minutes. I'll be as

     _____.

13. I can't see anything without my glasses on. I'm as _____.

14. What laundry detergent do you use? Your white shirts were covered with dirt, and now they're
    so clean and bright. They're as _____.

15. Shhh! Don't wake up Janet. She's sleeping on the couch. Be as _____.

16. Your little girl looks darling in that pink dress and hat. She looks as _____

     _____.

17. Don't worry. You'll pass the swimming test. It's not hard at all. It'll be as

     _____ for you.

18. Charles looks so relaxed since he quit his job. He has no responsibilities for now. He must feel

    as _____.

19. I have back problems and need to sleep on a bed that has a very firm mattress. My husband
    can sleep on anything, even something that is as _____.

20. It hasn't rained in weeks. The grass is brown, and the flowers are dead. The ground is as

     _____.

▶ **Practice 5. Comparative and superlative forms.** (Charts 9-2 and 9-3)
Write the comparative and superlative forms of the given words.

		COMPARATIVE		SUPERLATIVE	
1.	strong	_stronger_ than	the strongest	of all.
2.	important	_more important_ than	the most important	of all.
3.	soft	_____ than	_____	of all.
4.	lazy	_____ than	_____	of all.
5.	wonderful	_____ than	_____	of all.
6.	calm	_____ than	_____	of all.
7.	tame	_____ than	_____	of all.
8.	dim	_____ than	_____	of all.
9.	convenient	_____ than	_____	of all.
10.	clever	_____ than	_____	of all.
11.	good	_____ than	_____	of all.
12.	bad	_____ than	_____	of all.
13.	far	_____ than	_____	of all.

14. slow _____ than _____ of all.

15. slowly _____ than _____ of all.

▶ **Practice 6. Comparative forms.** (Charts 9-2 and 9-3)
Complete each sentence with the correct comparative form of the word in parentheses.

1. My mother is a few years (*old*) _____ my father.

2. An airplane is (*expensive*) _____ a car.

3. Which is (*large*) _____: Greenland or Iceland?

4. Red or cayenne pepper tastes (*hot*) _____ black pepper.

5. A typewriter is (*slow*) _____ a computer.

6. White chocolate is (*creamy*) _____ dark chocolate because it has more fat.

7. Is smoking (*bad*) _____ alcohol for your health?

8. A jaguar is (*fast*) _____ a lion.

9. Which is (*important*) _____: happiness or wealth?

10. For long-distance trips, flying is (*quick*) _____ driving or taking a train.

11. Which is (*heavy*) _____: a kilo of cotton or a kilo of rocks?*

12. Driving in a car equipped with a seat belt and an airbag is (*safe*) _____ driving in a car with just a seat belt.

13. Calculus is (*difficult*) _____ arithmetic.

▶ **Practice 7. Comparatives.** (Charts 9-2 and 9-3)
Complete the sentences with the correct comparative form of the words from the list.

cheap	dry	foggy	high	sunny
cold	expensive	healthy	international	

1. Locations near the equator are hot. Locations near the North Pole and the South Pole are cold. For example, Siberia is much _____ Cuba. The average temperature in Cuba is a lot _____ than the average temperature in Siberia.

2. Some places in northern Europe are often foggy. London is famous for its fog. It's much _____ in London, for example, than it is in southern Europe. The island of Majorca, in southern Spain, is very sunny. It's a lot _____ in Majorca than it is in London.

---

*This is a trick question.
Answer: They weigh the same.

3. Some people with illnesses have to move to places where there is dry air. For example, my uncle had to move to Arizona because the air there is a lot _____ than it is in Chicago, where he lived. The air in Arizona was good for him, and he became a lot _____ there.

4. New York is an international city. My hometown is just a small town. New York is much _____ than my hometown. It's expensive to live in New York. It's far _____ to live in New York than it is to live in my hometown. It's much _____ to live in my hometown than it is to live in New York.

▶ **Practice 8. Comparatives.** (Charts 9-2 and 9-3)
The given sentences contain words from Column A. Column B has words with the opposite meaning. Complete the sentences with the correct comparative form of the words in Column B.

Column A	Column B
careless	careful
uncomfortable	comfortable
lazy	energetic
stingy	generous
noisy, noisily	quiet, quietly
quiet, quietly	noisy, noisily
poor	rich
ugly	✓pretty

1. The James family painted their house. It was an ugly brown, but now it's a bright yellow. The house is much _____prettier_____ than it was before.

2. Jenny, that was very careless! You have to learn to be _____ with your things.

3. I love this cool weather. I don't feel lazy anymore. I feel _____ than I felt in the hot weather.

4. I felt very uncomfortable in the hot weather. I feel much _____ in this cool weather.

5. My parents are not stingy at all, but Frank's parents are stingy. My parents are _____ than Frank's parents.

6. Frank's parents are not poor. They are _____ than my parents.

7. In a library, some students are noisy, but most work _____. I can do a lot of work in a _____ place.

8. Our dog is big and noisy, but our new, little kitten is very soft and _____. Our dog is _____ than our cat. He walks _____ than our cat, he eats _____, and even sleeps _____. He snores!

▶ **Practice 9. Comparatives and superlatives.** (Charts 9-2 and 9-3)
Complete the sentences with *better*, *the best*, *worse*, or *the worst*.

1. I just finished a terrible book. It's _____*the worst*_____ book I've ever read.

2. The weather was bad yesterday, but it's terrible today. The weather is _____*worse*_____ today than it was yesterday.

3. This cake is really good. It's _____ cake I've ever eaten.

4. My grades this term are great. They're much _____ than last term.

5. Being separated from my family in time of war is one of _____ experiences I can imagine.

6. I broke my nose in a football game yesterday. Today it's very painful. For some reason, the pain is _____ today than it was yesterday.

7. The fire spread and burned down an entire city block. It was _____ fire we've ever had in our town.

8. I think my cold is almost over. I feel a lot _____ than I did yesterday. I can finally breathe again.

▶ **Practice 10. *Farther* and *Further*.** (Chart 9-3)
Choose the correct answer(s).

1. The planet Earth is _____ from the sun than the planet Mercury is.
   a. farther   b. further

2. I have no _____ need of this equipment. I'm going to sell it.
   a. farther   b. further

3. I'm tired. I walked _____ than I wanted to.
   a. farther   b. further

4. I'll be available by phone if you have any _____ questions.
   a. farther   b. further

5. A: Tell us more.
   B: Sorry, I have no _____ comment.
      a. farther   b. further

6. A: I heard that you and Tom are engaged to be married.
   B: Nothing could be _____ from the truth!
      a. farther   b. further

▶ **Practice 11. Adjectives vs. adverbs in the comparative.** (Chart 9-3)
Write the correct comparative form of the adjective or adverb in each sentence. If the word is an adjective, circle ADJ If it is an adverb, circle ADV.

1. *slow*   I like to drive fast, but my brother William doesn't. As a rule, he drives
   slowly   _____*more slowly*_____ than I do.   ADJ (ADV)

2. *slow*
   slowly
   Alex is a _____slower_____ driver than I am. (ADJ) ADV

3. *serious*
   seriously
   Some workers are _____ about their jobs than others.   ADJ   ADV

4. *serious*
   seriously
   Some workers approach their jobs _____ than others.   ADJ   ADV

5. *polite*
   politely
   Why is it that my children behave _____ at other people's houses than at home?   ADJ   ADV

6. *polite*
   politely
   Why are they _____ at Mrs. Miranda's house than at home?   ADJ   ADV

7. *careful*
   carefully
   I'm a cautious person when I express my opinions, but my sister will say anything to anyone. I'm much _____ when I speak to others than my sister is.   ADJ   ADV

8. *careful*
   carefully
   I always speak _____ in public than my sister does.   ADJ   ADV

9. *clear*
   clearly
   I can't understand Mark's father very well when he talks, but I can understand Mark. He speaks much _____ than his father.
   ADJ   ADV

10. *clear*
    clearly
    Mark is a much _____ speaker than his father.   ADJ   ADV

▶ **Practice 12. Completing comparisons with pronouns.** (Chart 9-4)
Complete the sentences with a pronoun and the correct auxiliary verb. Use both formal and informal completions.

1. Bob arrived at ten. I arrived at eleven.

   He arrived earlier than _____I did_____ / _____me_____ .

2. Linda is a good painter. Steven is better.

   He is a better painter than _____she is_____ / _____her_____ .

3. I won the race. Anna came in second.

   I ran faster than _____ / _____ .

4. My parents were nervous about my motorcycle ride. I was just a little nervous.

   They were a lot more nervous than _____ / _____ .

5. My aunt will stay with us for two weeks. My uncle has to return home to his job after a couple of days.

   She will be here with us a lot longer than _____ / _____ .

6. I've been here for two years. Sam has been here for two months.

   I've been here a lot longer than _____ / _____ .

7. I have a brother. His name is David. He's really tall. I'm just medium height.

   He's taller than _____ / _____ .

8. My brother is sixteen. I'm seventeen.

I'm older than _____ / _____.

9. My sister is really pretty. I've never thought I was pretty.

She's a lot prettier than _____ / _____.

10. I'm quite smart, though. My sister isn't interested in school.

I'm smarter than _____ / _____.

▶ **Practice 13. Very vs. a lot / much / far.** (Chart 9-5)
Circle the correct answer. More than one answer may be correct.

1. This watch is not _____ expensive.
   a. very   b. a lot   c. much   d. far

2. That watch is _____ more expensive than this one.
   a. very   b. a lot   c. much   d. far

3. My nephew is _____ polite.
   a. very   b. a lot   c. much   d. far

4. My nephew is _____ more polite than my niece.
   a. very   b. a lot   c. much   d. far

5. Ted is _____ taller than his brother.
   a. very   b. a lot   c. much   d. far

6. Ted is _____ tall.
   a. very   b. a lot   c. much   d. far

7. I think astronomy is _____ more interesting than geology.
   a. very   b. a lot   c. much   d. far

8. I think astronomy is _____ interesting.
   a. very   b. a lot   c. much   d. far

9. It took me a lot longer to get over my cold than it took you to get over your cold. My cold was
   _____ worse than yours.
   a. very   b. a lot   c. much   d. far

▶ **Practice 14. Not as . . . as and less . . . than.** (Chart 9-6)
The passage contains nine phrases with **not as . . . (as)**. Underline these phrases, and if possible, change them to sentences with the same meaning using **less . . . (than)**.

A Move to a New Town

(1) Lia has been unhappy ever since she and her family moved to Southland, a suburb of a big city. She was very happy with her life in the city, where she had lived since she was born. She liked her friends, her school, and her neighborhood there.

(2) In her new school, the students are <u>not as friendly as</u> her old schoolmates. The classes are not as interesting as the ones in her old school, and she is a little bored. The classes are not as difficult, and she feels that she isn't learning much.

(3) She doesn't like her new neighborhood. It is not as convenient as her old neighborhood. In the city, all the stores were near her home. In the suburbs, the stores are not as close to her home as they were in the city. In the city, she didn't have to travel far to shop or go to a movie. Lia also misses the cultural events of the city. The cultural life in Southland is not as exciting as it is in the city, where she often went to concerts, plays, and interesting lectures.

(4) Lia is not as comfortable with her life now as she used to be. But, she is not as unhappy as she was at first. She is working on changing her attitude. She is hoping that with time, she will find that life in Southland is not as bad as she thought.

9-A Unclear Comparisons

UNCLEAR (a) Ann likes her dog better than her husband.	Sometimes it is necessary to complete the idea following ***than*** in order to make a comparison clear.
CLEAR (b) Ann likes her dog better than her husband does. (c) Ann likes her dog better than she does her husband.	In (b): *does* means "likes the dog." In (c): *does* means "likes."

▶ **Practice 15. Unclear comparisons.** (Chart 9-A)
Read the given sentence. Then choose all the sentences that are true.

1. Jana likes tennis more than her husband.
   - (a.) Jana likes tennis.
   - (b.) Jana might not like her husband.
   - (c.) Jana's husband doesn't like tennis as much as Jana does.

2. Jana likes tennis more than her husband does.
   - a. Jana likes tennis.
   - b. Jana might not like her husband.
   - c. Jana's husband doesn't like tennis as much as Jana does.

3. Franco helped me more than Debra.
   - a. Franco didn't help Debra very much.
   - b. Debra didn't help me very much.
   - c. Franco was helpful to me.

4. Franco helped me more than Debra did.
   a. Franco didn't help Debra very much.
   b. Debra didn't help me very much.
   c. Franco was helpful to me.

5. I pay my plumber more than my dentist.
   a. My plumber is more expensive than my dentist.
   b. My dentist doesn't pay the plumber as much as I do.
   c. I pay only my plumber, not my dentist.

6. I pay my plumber more than I pay my dentist.
   a. My plumber is more expensive than my dentist.
   b. My dentist doesn't pay the plumber as much as I do.
   c. I pay only my plumber, not my dentist.

▶ **Practice 16. Unclear comparisons.** (Chart 9-A)
Check (✓) the sentences that have unclear comparisons. Make the necessary corrections.

1. __✓__ Sam enjoys football more than his best friend *does*.

2. _____ Andy writes better financial reports than his boss.

3. _____ The coach helped Anna more than Nancy.

4. _____ Sara likes tennis more than her husband.

5. _____ Cathy leaves more generous tips at restaurants than her husband.

6. _____ Kelly eats more organic food than his roommate.

7. _____ Charles knows Judy better than Kevin.

▶ **Practice 17. Using *more* with nouns.** (Chart 9-7)
Complete each sentence with a word from the list. Use *more* to make the comparison.

books	enjoyment	readers
cell phones	news	things

1. There are _____ in the public library than there are in my home. I have a few hundred, but the library has thousands.

2. A lot of people download books onto their computers or other devices. I prefer to hold a book, though. I get _____ from holding a real book than I do from reading one on a computer.

3. People read _____ on their computers than they do in newspapers

4. In fact, several big newspapers have closed down. The newspapers used to have many _____ than they do now.

5. In many countries, there are a lot _____ than land lines. Phones in homes are less common than mobile phones.

6. A cell phone can do _____ than a land line can. For example, it can take pictures, keep a calendar, and even connect to the Internet.

▶ **Practice 18. Using _more_ with nouns and adjectives.** (Charts 9-3 and 9-8)

Part I. Adjectives
Complete the sentences with the correct comparative form (***more/-er***).

| difficult | loud | pleasant |

1. A warm, sunny day is _____ than a cold windy day.

2. Karen doesn't need a microphone when she speaks to the audience. She's the only person I know whose voice is _____ than mine.

3. My course in microbiology is much _____ than my biology course was.

Part II. Adverbs
Use the adverb forms of these adjectives.

| careful | clear | fast |

4. Your new phone is excellent, Joe. I can hear you much _____ on this phone than on your old one.

5. Aunt Anna has been driving _____ since she had her accident on the highway. In fact, she drives very slowly now, and she is quite nervous.

6. You can cook food in a microwave oven much _____ than you can cook it in a regular oven. It takes only seven minutes to bake a potato, for example.

Part III. Nouns
Use the plural form of these nouns if necessary.

| car | friend | homework | money | problem | snow |

7. University students study hard. They have a lot _____ than high school students.

8. There is far _____ in winter in Alaska than there is in Texas.

9. I'm lonely. I wish I had _____ to spend time with.

10. Sam's car is ten years old. He has _____ with it than he did when it was new.

11. Traffic in this city has become a big problem. There are many _____ on the road now than there were five years ago.

12. The economy is improving in this area. Small businesses made _____ this year than they did last year.

▶ **Practice 19. Repeating a comparative.** (Chart 9-8)
Complete the sentences with words from the list. Repeat the comparative.

bad	big	expensive	friendly	✓good	long	mad	noisy	warm

1. His health is improving. He's getting _____ *better and better* _____.

2. The Davidsons just had their sixth child. Their family is getting

   _____.

3. People are worried about the environment. The ice at the North and South poles is melting because the earth is getting _____.

4. This neighborhood used to be quiet, but since a new mall opened nearby, it is getting

   _____.

5. I was really angry! I got _____ until my brother touched my arm and told me to calm down.

6. We were so glad we had arrived early at the ticket office. As we waited for it to open, the line got _____.

7. Textbooks are costly. They are getting _____ every year.

8. When Maya first came into our class, she was very shy. She didn't talk to anyone. But little by little, she has relaxed, and now she is getting _____.

9. The weather is getting _____. The airport has canceled most flights because of the snowstorm.

▶ **Practice 20. Double comparatives.** (Chart 9-9)
Complete the sentences with double comparatives.

1. I exercise every day. Exercise makes me strong. The _____ *more* _____ I exercise, the
   _____ *stronger* _____ I get.

2. If butter is soft, it is easy to spread on bread. The _____ the butter is, the _____ it is to spread on bread.

3. I'm trying to make my life simpler. It makes me feel more relaxed.
   The _____ I make my life, the _____ I feel.

4. I spend a long time each day looking at a computer screen. My eyes get very tired.
   The _____ I look at a computer screen, the
   _____ my eyes get.

5. When the wind blows hard, it whistles through the trees.
   The _____ the wind blows, the _____ it
   whistles through the trees.

► **Practice 21. Double comparatives.** (Chart 9-9)
Complete the sentences with double comparatives, using the ideas in parentheses.

1. (*She talked. She got excited.*)

   I met a woman at a party last night. She told us many stories about her exciting job as a

   wildlife photographer. The _____, _____.

2. (*He talked. I got hungry.*)

   I also met a man who is a chef. He talked about some of the great meals he makes. I got

   hungry just listening to him. The _____, _____.

3. (*You understand more. You are old.*)

   There are many advantages to being young, but the _____,

   _____.

4. (*Bill talked very fast. I became confused.*)

   Bill was trying to explain some complicated physics problems to help me prepare for an exam.

   He kept talking faster and faster. The _____,

   _____.

5. (*The fans clapped and cheered. The basketball team made more shots.*)

   The fans in the arena were excited and noisy, and it seemed to make their team play better.

   The _____,

   _____.

► **Practice 22. Using superlatives.** (Chart 9-10)
Complete the sentences with the given ideas and the superlative form.

bad flood	far planet	intelligent animals
big organ	good policy	popular sport
common word	high level	tall mountain

1. Mount McKinley in Alaska is the _____ in North America.
2. The skin is _____ in the human body. It covers the largest area.
3. *The* is _____ in the English language.
4. Neptune is _____ from the sun.
5. _____ in the world is football.
6. Bottle-nosed dolphins are _____ that live in the water.

$E = MC^2$

7. Last spring, the towns on the river experienced _____ of this century. The water rose to _____ that it ever had in the towns' history.

8. A famous proverb, and a rule for living, is "Honesty is _____." It means that you should always be honest.

▶ **Practice 23. Using superlatives.** (Chart 9-10)
Part I. Complete the sentences with superlatives and the appropriate word: *in*, *of*, or *ever*.

1. Economics is (*difficult*) _____the most difficult_____ course I have _____ever_____ taken.

2. For me, English is (*easy*) _____ course I have _____ taken.

3. A lot of students take a course called *The History of Rap Music* because it is one of (*interesting*) _____ courses _____ the college.

4. The professor who teaches it is excellent. He is one of (*good*) _____ professors _____ all the professors in the college.

5. My friends say that my grandmother is (*wise*) _____ person they have _____ met.

6. My wife won our town's annual marathon race twice. She was (*fast*) _____ runner _____ all.

7. My three children all have artistic talent, but Jimmy is (*artistic*) _____ _____ all.

8. My cousin Carolina has won a scholarship to Harvard University to study mathematics. She is one of (*brilliant*) _____ mathematics students _____ the whole country.

9. One of (*successful*) _____ business people _____ our town is Mitchell Brown, the owner of our only independent bookstore.

10. He established the store ten years ago, and now it is (*busy*) _____ bookstore _____ our area.

11. Mitchell is not only a successful businessperson, but he is one of (*generous*) _____ people that our town has _____ known. He has given a lot of time and money to local charities.

12. Mitchell believes that contributing to the quality of life in his community is (*important*) _____ thing that he can do _____ life.

Part II. Make comparisons using *the least* with the word in parentheses, and *in*, *of*, or *ever*.

13. Ed is not lazy, but he is certainly (*ambitious*) _____the least ambitious of_____ all the people I have worked with.

14. That painting didn't cost much. It is (*expensive*) _____ work of art we have _____ bought.

15. Antarctica is (*populated*) _____ continent _____ the world.

16. Kim is never tense or nervous. She is (*anxious*) _____ person that I have _____ known. She is always calm.

► **Practice 24. As . . . as, more / -er, and most / -est.** (Charts 9-1 → 9-10)

Part I. Compare the cost of the items in parentheses. Use the given expressions.

1. (*a pencil vs.* a phone*)

   _____*A pencil*_____ is less expensive than _____*a phone*_____.

2. (*a paper clip vs. a diamond ring*)

   _____ is much more expensive than _____.

3. (*a cup of coffee vs. a bag of coffee beans*)

   _____ is not as expensive as _____.

4. (*radios vs. MP3 players vs. big screen TVs*)

   _____ and _____ are both less expensive

   than _____.

5. (*a compact car vs. a house*)

   _____ is not nearly as expensive as _____.

6. (*footballs vs. soccer balls vs. table-tennis balls vs. basketballs*)

   _____, _____, and

   _____ are all more expensive than _____.

Part II. Compare the waterfalls by using the given expressions.

7. _____*Angel Falls*_____ is much higher _____*than Niagara Falls***_____.

8. _____ is almost as high _____.

9. _____ is the highest _____.

10. _____ is not nearly as high _____.

11. _____ is not quite as high _____.

Waterfalls of the World

Niagara Falls	Giessbach Falls	Cuquenán Falls	Angel Falls
United States and Canada	Switzerland	Venezuela	Venezuela
53 meters	604 meters	610 meters	807 meters

**vs.* is an abbreviation for *versus*, which means "as opposed to, as compared to."

**A singular verb is used after Angel Falls because it is the name of a place. Angel Falls is in Venezuela. Similarly, the United States takes a singular verb because it is the name of a place: *The United States is a big country.*

Part III. Compare the weight of the items in parentheses. Use the given expressions.

12. (*air, iron*) _____Air_____ is lighter _____than iron_____.

13. (*iron, wood*) _____ is heavier _____.

14. (*water, iron, wood, air*) Of the four elements, _____ is the heaviest

_____.

15. (*water, air*) _____ is not as heavy _____.

16. (*water, iron, wood, air*) Of the four elements, _____ is the lightest

_____.

17. (*water, air*) _____ is not nearly as light _____.

18. (*water, iron, wood*) _____ and _____ are both heavier

_____.

▶ **Practice 25. Using *never* with comparatives.** (Chart 9-10)
Choose the sentence that is closest in meaning to the given sentence.

1. I've never taken a harder test in this class.
   (a.) The test was hard.
   b. The test wasn't hard.

2. I've never taken a hard test in this class.
   a. The tests in this class are hard.
   b. The tests in this class aren't hard.

3. Professor Jones has never given a difficult test.
   a. His tests are difficult.
   b. His tests aren't difficult.

4. Professor Smith has never given a more difficult test.
   a. The test was difficult.
   b. The test wasn't difficult.

5. There have never been worse economic conditions in Leadville.
   a. Leadville has bad economic conditions.
   b. Leadville doesn't have bad economic conditions.

6. There have never been bad economic conditions in Leadville.
   a. Leadville has bad economic conditions.
   b. Leadville doesn't have bad economic conditions.

7. We've never stayed in a more comfortable hotel room.
   a. The room was comfortable.
   b. The room wasn't comfortable.

8. We've never stayed in a comfortable room at that hotel.
   a. The rooms are comfortable.
   b. The rooms aren't comfortable.

▶ **Practice 26. Using *ever* and *never* in comparisons.** (Charts 9-3 and 9-10)
Complete the sentences with the comparative and superlative forms of the words in *italics*.

1. Pierre told a really *funny* story. It is _____*the funniest*_____ story I've ever heard (in my life). I've never heard a _____*funnier*_____ story (than that one).

2. John felt very *sad* when he saw the child begging for money. In fact, he has never felt _____ (than he did then). That is _____ he has ever felt (in his life).

3. Jan just finished a really *good* book. She thinks it was _____ book she has ever read. She says that she has never read a _____ book.

4. The villagers fought the rising flood all through the night. They were *exhausted* the next morning. They have never had a _____ experience. That was _____ experience they have ever had.

5. When her daughter was born, Rachel felt extremely *happy*. In fact, she has never felt _____ (than she did then). That was _____ she has ever felt (in her life).

6. Oscar told a very *entertaining* story after dinner. In fact, he has never told a _____ _____ story. It is one of _____ stories I have ever heard in my life.

7. Mari studied very *hard* for her college entrance exams. In fact, she has never studied _____. That was _____ she has ever studied in her life.

8. The weather is really *hot* today! In fact, so far this year the weather has never been _____. This is _____ weather we've had so far this year.

▶ **Practice 27. Review of comparatives and superlatives.** (Charts 9-1 → 9-10)
Choose the correct completion.

1. I feel _____ in a plane than I do in a car.
   a. safe   b. more safer   c. safer

2. Mountain climbing takes _____ than walking on a level path.
   a. the more strength   b. the most strength   c. more strength

3. The _____ distance between two points is a straight line.
   a. shorter   b. more shorter   c. shortest

4. My grandfather feels _____ speaking his native language than he does speaking English.
   a. more comfortable   b. the more comfortable   c. the most comfortable

5. My friend has studied many languages. He thinks Japanese is _____ of all the languages he has studied.
   a. the more difficult   b. the most difficult   c. very difficult

6. I think learning a second language is _____ than learning chemistry or mathematics.
   a. more difficult   b. very difficult   c. the most difficult

7. One of _____ natural disasters in the world was the tsunami that happened in Asia in 2004.
   a. the worse   b. the worst   c. the most worse

8. In the United States, Florida produces _____ oranges of any state.
   a. more   b. the more   c. the most

9. It produces even _____ oranges than California does.
   a. more   b. the more   c. the most

10. Of all the countries in the world, Brazil produces _____ crop of oranges.
    a. the bigger   b. the more bigger   c. the biggest

▶ **Practice 28. Review of comparatives and superlatives.** (Charts 9-1 → 9-10)
Complete the sentences. Use any appropriate form of the words in parentheses and add any other necessary words.

1. Sometimes I feel like all of my friends are (*intelligent*) _____*more intelligent than*_____ I am, and yet, sometimes they tell me that they think I am (*smart*) _____*the smartest*_____ person __*in*__ the class.

2. One of (*popular*) _____ holidays _____ Japan is New Year's.

3. A mouse is (*small*) _____ a rat.

4. Europe is first in agricultural production of potatoes. (*potatoes*) _____ are grown in Europe _____ on any other continent.

5. Mercury is (*close*) _____ planet to the sun. It moves around the sun (*fast*) _____ any other planet in the solar system.

6. In terms of area, (*large*) _____ state _____ the United States is Alaska, but it has one of (*small*) _____ populations _____ all the states.

7. I need more facts. I can't make my decision until I get (*information*) _____ _____.

8. Rebecca is a wonderful person. I don't think I've ever met a (*kind*) _____ and (*generous*) _____ person.

9. You can trust Rebecca. You will never meet a (*honest*) _____ person _____ she is.

10. I'm leaving. This is (*bad*) _____ movie I've ever seen! I won't sit through another second of it.

11. One of (*safe*) _____ places to be during a lightning storm is inside a car.

12. Small birds have a much (*fast*) _____ heartbeat _____ large birds.

13. Are your feet exactly the same size? Almost everyone's left foot is (*big*) _____ their right foot.*

---

*Grammar note: In formal English, a singular pronoun is used to refer to *everyone*:
    Almost **everyone's** left foot is bigger than **his or her** right foot.
In everyday informal usage, a plural pronoun is frequently used:
    Almost **everyone's** left foot is bigger than **their** right foot.

► **Practice 29. _Like, alike._** (Chart 9-11)
Complete the sentences with **_like_** or **_alike_**.

1. My mother and my father rarely argue because they think _____*alike*_____.

2. The Browns designed their summer cabin to look _____*like*_____ the inside of a boat.

3. Joe and John are twins, but they don't look _____.

4. They dress _____ because they have the same taste in clothes.

5. This lamp doesn't look _____ the one I ordered.

6. Mike is 30, but he acts _____ a child.

7. Professor Miller's lectures are all _____: repetitive and boring.

8. This coffee doesn't taste _____ the coffee we sampled at the store.

9. The clouds in the east look _____ rain clouds.

10. My grandmother and mother sound _____ on the phone.

► **Practice 30. _The same, similar, different._** (Chart 9-11)
Complete the sentences with **_the same_**, **_similar_**, or **_different_** and the correct preposition: **_as, to,_** or **_from_**.

1. My coat is not like yours. It's _____*different from*_____ yours.

2. Our apartment is a lot like my cousin's apartment. It's _____ hers.

3. The news report on Channel 4 at 7:00 P.M. was exactly _____ the report we heard on Channel 6 at 6:00 P.M.

4. Is the North Pole really _____ the South Pole? I thought they were exactly alike.

5. Your jacket is just like mine. It's exactly _____ mine.

6. I enjoyed reading your letters from China. My experiences in Beijing were a lot like yours. They were _____ yours in many ways.

7. The movie on our flight to London was _____ the movie on our flight to Paris. The name of the movie was _Forever Lost_.

8. Except for some minor differences in grammar, spelling, and vocabulary, American English is _____ British English. It's one language.

9. The English spoken in the United States is only slightly _____ the English spoken in Britain, Canada, and Australia. The most noticeable difference is the accent.

10. Lemons are _____ limes. They both taste sour.

11. My sisters are twins, but they are very _____ each other. They don't even look alike.

► **Practice 31. Like, alike, similar, different.** (Chart 9-11)
Part I. Compare the figures using the given words.

A   B   C   D

1. like _____A is like D_____.

2. alike _____.

3. similar (to) _____ and _____.

4. different (from) _____, _____, and _____.

Part II. Compare the figures. Use *the same* (*as*), *similar* (*to*), or *different* (*from*).

A   B   C   D

5. All of the triangles are _____ each other.

6. A and D are _____ each other.

7. A and C are _____.

8. A isn't _____ C.

9. B and C are _____ D.

► **Practice 32. The same, similar, different, like, alike.** (Chart 9-11)
Complete the sentences with *the same, similar, different, like,* or *alike*.

1. Dana swims _____*like*_____ a fish. She never wants to come out of the water.

2. The lake doesn't have a ripple on it. It looks _____ glass.

3. There are six girls in our family, but none of us look _____. Our brothers also

   look different.

4. A: Some people can tell we're sisters. Do you think we look _____?

   B: Somewhat. The color of your hair is not _____, but your eyes are exactly

   _____ color. You also have _____ oval face.

5. A: Excuse me. I believe you have my umbrella.

   B: Oh, you're right. It looks almost exactly _____ mine, doesn't it?

6. A: This pasta is delicious! It tastes just _____ the pasta we had in Italy.

   B: Well, not exactly. It's _____ to the pasta in Italy, but it's not as good.

7. Some people think my sister and I are twins. We look _____ and talk
   _____, but our personalities are quite _____.

8. Homonyms are words that have _____ pronunciation but different spelling,
   such as "pair" and "pear" or "sea" and "see." For many people, "been" and "bean" are
   homonyms and have _____ pronunciation. For other people, however, "been"
   and "bean" are words with _____ pronunciations. These people pronounce
   "been" like "bin" or "ben."

▶ **Practice 33. Editing.** (Chapter 9)
Correct the errors.

1. My brother is older ~~from~~ *than* me.

2. A sea is more deeper than a lake.

3. A donkey isn't as big to a horse.

4. Ellen is happiest person I've ever met.

5. When I feel embarrassed, my face gets hot and more hot.

6. One of a largest animal in the world is the hippopotamus.

7. The traffic on the highway is more bad from than it used to be.

8. Jack is the same old from Jerry.

9. Peas are similar from beans, but they have several differences.

10. Last winter was pretty mild. This winter is cold and rainy. It's much rain than last winter.

11. Mrs. Peters, the substitute teacher, is very friendly than the regular instructor.

12. Although alligators and crocodiles are similar, alligators are less big than crocodiles.

13. Mohammed and Tarek come from different countries, but they became friends easily because
    they speak a same language, Arabic.

► Practice 34. Crossword puzzle. (Chapter 9)

Complete the crossword puzzle. Use the clues to find the correct words.

Across

2. My husband is a good cook, but my mother is the _____ cook in the world.

6. A turtle walks more _____ than a rabbit.

8. The weather is really bad this summer. It rains all the time, and the heat is terrible. It's the _____ summer we've ever had.

9. Arithmetic is _____ than advanced calculus.

10. I have a bad cold. I went to work, but that was a mistake. I had to go home early. I feel even _____ than I did this morning.

Down

1. Kim speaks English much _____ than he did last year.

3. We are taking the _____ plane tomorrow morning. It leaves at 6:00 A.M.

4. The _____ swimmer won first prize.

5. Many people think that Paris is the _____ beautiful city in the world.

7. There are _____ letters in the word *happy* than in the word *sad*.

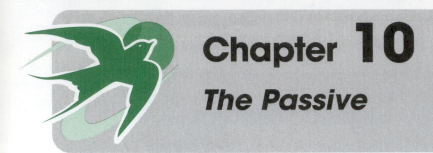

Chapter 10
The Passive

▶ **Practice 1. Active vs. passive.** (Charts 10-1 and 10-2)
Circle *active* if the given sentence is active; circle *passive* if it is passive. Underline the verb.

1. (active)   passive   Farmers <u>grow</u> rice.
2. active   (passive)   Rice <u>is grown</u> by farmers.
3. active   passive   Sara wrote the letter.
4. active   passive   The letter was written by Sara.
5. active   passive   The teacher explained the lesson.
6. active   passive   The lesson was explained by the teacher.
7. active   passive   Bridges are designed by engineers.
8. active   passive   Engineers design bridges.
9. active   passive   Workers are fixing the highway.
10. active   passive   The highway is being fixed by workers.

▶ **Practice 2. Active vs. passive.** (Charts 10-1 and 10-2)
Change the active verbs in *italics* to passive.

1. Mr. Case *delivers* our mail every day.   Our mail ____*is delivered*____ by Mr. Case every day.

2. Mr. Case *is delivering* our mail right now.   Our mail _____ by Mr. Case right now.

3. Mr. Case *has delivered* our mail for ten years.   Our mail _____ by Mr. Case for ten years.

4. Mr. Case *delivered* our mail early today.   Our mail _____ by Mr. Case early today.

5. Mr. Case *was delivering* our mail when a loud explosion occurred.   Our mail _____ by Mr. Case when a loud explosion occurred.

6. Mr. Case *is going to deliver* our mail late today.   Our mail _____ by Mr. Case late today.

7. Mr. Case *will deliver* the mail early on Saturday.   Our mail _____ by Mr. Case early on Saturday.

► **Practice 3. Forms of the passive.** (Charts 10-1 and 10-2)
Choose the correct completion from the list for each sentence.

Present
   a. are flown
   b. are led
   c. is grown
   d. is followed

  1. Coffee __c__ in hot climates.
  2. Planes _____ by pilots.
  3. Armies _____ by generals.
  4. The month of May _____ by the month of June.

Past
   e. was bitten
   f. was discovered
   g. were shot
   h. were made

  5. I _____ by a mosquito.
  6. The bears _____ by hunters.
  7. These cookies _____ by my grandmother.
  8. Penicillin _____ by Alexander Fleming, a Scottish scientist.

Future
   i. are going to be elected
   j. is going to be sent
   k. will be taken
   l. will be won

  9. The wedding photos _____ by a professional photographer.
 10. A new president and vice-president _____ by the people.
 11. The gold medal _____ by the fastest runner.
 12. This package _____ by overnight mail. You'll receive it tomorrow.

Present perfect
  m. has been bought
  n. has been written
  o. have been arrested
  p. have been invited

 13. I _____ by the governor to attend a special conference.
 14. A book about our town _____ by my sociology professor.
 15. The house next to ours _____ by an airline pilot.
 16. Two men _____ by the police for robbing the bank last month.

Progressive
  q. are being taught
  r. is being chased
  s. was being served
  t. were being carried

 17. Look at that. That little dog _____ by that big cat!
 18. The children _____ French by a native French speaker.
 19. Dinner _____ at the restaurant when the lights suddenly went out.
 20. We saw scenes of the fire on TV. People _____ from the burning building by fire fighters.
      Fortunately, no one died in the fire.

▶ Practice 4. Review of past participles. (Charts 2-3 and 2-4)

Write the past participles of the verbs. The list contains both regular and irregular verbs.

1. bring _____brought_____
2. build _____
3. buy _____
4. carry _____
5. do _____
6. eat _____
7. find _____
8. give _____
9. go _____
10. grow _____
11. hit _____
12. hurt _____
13. leave _____
14. lose _____

15. make _____
16. plan _____
17. play _____
18. pull _____
19. read _____
20. save _____
21. send _____
22. speak _____
23. spend _____
24. take _____
25. teach _____
26. visit _____
27. wear _____
28. write _____

▶ Practice 5. Passive form. (Charts 10-1 and 10-2)

Complete the sentences with the given form of *be* and the past participle of any appropriate verbs in the list in Practice 4.

1. *is*   Arabic _____ by more than 800 million people.

2. *are*   Books _____ by authors.

3. *are*   Books _____ by readers.

4. *was*   A new school _____ in our town last year.

5. *were*   The two lost children _____ at the ice cream shop.

6. *has been*   There's no more pizza. All the pizza _____ by the
                 kids.

7. *is going to be*   Niagara Falls _____ by thousands of tourists
                      this year.

8. *will be*   The championship football game _____ in Milan
                 next week.

9. *are going to be* Our pictures _____ by a professional
                      photographer at the wedding.

10. *have been* Oranges _____ by farmers in Jordan since
                 ancient times.

11. *are being* Jeans _____ by everyone these days: young
                 people, old people, men, and women.

12. *was being*   Yesterday I saw something unusual on the highway. A house

_____ by a truck.

▶ **Practice 6. Tense forms of the passive.** (Charts 10-1 and 10-2)
Complete the sentences with the passive form of the given verbs.

Part I. Use the <u>simple present</u>.

✓collect	grow	understand
eat	pay	write

1. Taxes _____are collected_____ by the government.

2. Books _____ by authors.

3. Rice _____ by farmers in Korea.

4. Small fish _____ by big fish.

5. I _____ for my work by my boss.

6. The meaning of a smile _____ by everyone.

Part II. Use the <u>simple past</u>.

build	✓collect	destroy	write

7. Yesterday the students' papers _____were collected_____ by the teacher at the end of the test.

8. The Great Wall of China _____ by Chinese emperors more than 2,500 years ago.

9. The *Harry Potter* books _____ by J. K. Rowling, a former English teacher.

10. An office building in Jakarta _____ by the earthquake.

Part III. Use the <u>present perfect</u>.

> read   speak   ✓visit   wear

11. The pyramids in Egypt _____*have been visited*_____ by millions of tourists.
12. Spanish _____ by people in Latin America for nearly 600 years.
13. *War and Peace* is a famous book. It _____ by millions of people.
14. Perfume _____ by both men and women since ancient times.

Part IV. Use <u>future</u> (***will***).

> ✓discover   save   visit

15. New information about the universe _____*will be discovered*_____ by scientists during this century.
16. Hawaii _____ by thousands of tourists this year.
17. Pandas _____ from extinction by the Chinese government and organizations like the World Wildlife Federation.

Part V. Use <u>future</u> (a form of ***be going to***).

> choose   ✓hurt   offer

18. Your friend _____*is going to be hurt*_____ by your unkind remark when she hears about it.
19. New computer courses _____ by the university next year.
20. The winner of the essay contest _____ by the English teachers of our school.

Part VI. Use ***am / is / are / was / were + being***.

> ✓announce   cover   follow   treat   wash

21. The scholarship winner _____*is being announced*_____ by the college president right now.
22. There's a big storm in the mountains right now. The roads _____ by ice and snow, and driving conditions are becoming dangerous.
23. I _____ by a headache specialist for my headaches. I see him every month.
24. In the spy movie we saw last night, the suspect _____ by the detective, but he moved faster than the detective and disappeared into the city.

25. Yesterday, while I was at work, a man suddenly appeared outside my office window. It took a few seconds for me to realize that the windows _____ by window washers.

▶ **Practice 7. Passive vs. active meaning.** (Charts 10-1 and 10-2)
Circle the letter of the sentence that has the same meaning as the given sentence.

1. My grandmother makes her own bread. Have a slice.
   a. This bread is made by my grandmother.
   b. Someone makes my grandmother's bread.

2. Bob was taken to the hospital by car.
   a. Bob drove to the hospital.
   b. Someone drove Bob to the hospital.

3. Suzanne has just been asked to her first dance.
   a. Suzanne has asked someone to the dance.
   b. Someone has asked Suzanne to the dance.

4. You will be informed of the test results.
   a. Someone will inform you of the test results.
   b. You will inform someone of the test results.

5. A sign: "You are not allowed to enter."
   a. You do not allow people to enter.
   b. Someone says you cannot enter.

6. The child was saved after five minutes in the water.
   a. Someone saved the child.
   b. The child saved herself.

7. An announcement on the phone: "For security purposes, this telephone conversation is being recorded."
   a. You are recording the phone conversation.
   b. Someone else is recording the telephone conversation.

▶ **Practice 8. Forms of passive questions.** (Charts 10-1 and 10-2)
Change the questions from active to passive.

1. Did many people see the game?

   _____Was the game seen by many people?_____

2. Will the news shock Pat?

   _____

3. Is the restaurant serving lunch now?

   _____

4. Does everyone understand the rules?

   _____

5. Is the professor going to explain the solution?

   _____

6. Has the university accepted you?

_____

7. Have both the seller and the buyer signed the contract?

_____

8. Did the police find the thief?

_____

▶ **Practice 9. Passive to active.** (Charts 10-1 and 10-2)
Rewrite the paragraph in the active voice. Keep the same tense.

Taxes are collected by governments. The tax money is used by the governments. Many services are provided by the tax money. These services are used by us regularly. For example: Roads are built and repaired by local workers. Police forces are trained by experts. The fire department is operated by the city. Teachers are paid by the county. Professional licenses are issued by the state. The postal system is run by the country. Armies are maintained by countries. Health care is managed by many governments.

Governments _____collect taxes_____. Governments _____.
                    1   2

The tax money _____. We _____
                        3   4

regularly. For example: Local workers _____. Experts
                                              5

_____. The city _____.
           6   7

The county _____. The state _____.
                    8   9

The country _____. Countries _____.
                     10   11

Many governments _____.
                          12

▶ **Practice 10. Passive to active.** (Charts 5-2, 10-1, and 10-2)
Change the passive sentences to active. Keep the same tense of each sentence. Some of the sentences are questions.

1. A new film from India, *Falling Rocks*, will be shown by the City Film Society.

    _____The City Film Society will show a new film from India, Falling Rocks._____

2. The film has been reviewed by movie critics.

    _____

3. The movie was given good ratings by audiences.

    _____

4. Was the movie written by a famous writer?

    _____

5. The main female part is played by a new actress.

    _____

6. Is a murder committed by someone in the movie?

    _____

7. Is the main character killed by a spy?

_____

8. Will the movie be seen by many people?

_____

9. Is an award going to be won by the movie?

_____

▶ **Practice 11. Transitive vs. intransitive.** (Chart 10-3)
Circle transitive if the verb takes an object; circle intransitive if it does not. <u>Underline</u> the object of the verb.

1. (transitive)   intransitive   Alex wrote <u>a letter</u>.

2. transitive   (intransitive)   Alex waited for Amy. (*There is no object of the verb.*)

3. transitive   intransitive   Rita lives in Mexico.

4. transitive   intransitive   Sam walked to his office.

5. transitive   intransitive   Kate caught the ball.

6. transitive   intransitive   My plane arrived at six-thirty.

7. transitive   intransitive   Emily is crying.

8. transitive   intransitive   Our cat broke the vase.

9. transitive   intransitive   Someone returned the book to the library.

10. transitive   intransitive   A meteor appeared in the sky last night.

▶ **Practice 12. Active and passive.** (Charts 10-1 → 10-3)
<u>Underline</u> the object of the verb if the sentence has one. Then change the sentence to the passive if possible.

Active	Passive
1. It was raining hard last night.	*No change* .
2. Around midnight, loud sounds awakened <u>me</u>.	*I was awakened by loud sounds around midnight* .
3. Lightning struck a tree.	_____ .
4. The tree fell down.	_____ .
5. The tree hit my neighbor's car.	_____ .
6. The impact activated the car alarm.	_____ .
7. The car alarm sounded very loud.	_____ .
8. The tree damaged the roof of the car.	_____ .
9. Fortunately, no one was inside the car.	_____ .
10. The damage is going to upset my neighbor.	_____ .

▶ **Practice 13. Review: identifying passives with transitive and intransitive verbs.**
(Charts 10-1 → 10-3)
Check (✓) the sentences that are passive.

1. _____ I came by plane.

2. _✓_ I was invited to the party by Alex.

3. _____ Many people died during the earthquake.

4. _____ Many people were killed by collapsing buildings.

5. _____ The earthquake has killed many people.

6. _____ The game will be won by the home team.

7. _____ The home team will win the game.

8. _____ Gina's baby cried for more than an hour.

9. _____ Most of the fresh fruit at the market was bought by customers.

10. _____ Some customers bought boxes full of fresh fruit.

11. _____ Accidents always occur at that intersection.

▶ **Practice 14. The *by*-phrase.** (Chart 10-4)
Underline the passive verbs. Answer the questions. If you don't know the exact person or people who performed the action, write *unknown*.

1. Soft duck feathers <u>are used</u> to make pillows.

   Who uses duck feathers to make pillows? _____*unknown*_____

2. The mail <u>was opened</u> by Shelley.

   Who opened the mail? _____*Shelley*_____

3. Eric Wong's new book will be translated into many languages.

   Who will translate Eric Wong's new book? _____

4. Rebecca's bike was stolen yesterday from in front of the library.

   Who stole Rebecca's bike? _____

5. The Warren's house was designed by a famous architect.

   Who designed the Warren's house? _____

6. Malawi is a small country in southeastern Africa. A new highway is going to be built in Malawi next year.

   Who is going to build the new highway? _____

7. There are no more empty apartments in our building. The apartment next to ours has been rented by a young family with two small children.

   Who rented the apartment next to ours? _____

8. The apartment directly above ours was empty for two months, but now it has also been rented.

   Who rented the apartment directly above ours? _____

► **Practice 15. Active to passive.** (Charts 10-1 → 10-4)
Change the active sentences to passive. Use the *by*-phrase only if necessary.

1. Someone has canceled the soccer game.

   The soccer game has been canceled.

2. The president has canceled the meeting.

   The meeting has been canceled by the president.

3. Someone serves ethnic dishes at that restaurant.

   _____

4. Something confused me in class yesterday.

   _____

5. The teacher's directions confused me.

   _____

6. No one has washed the dishes yet.

   _____

7. Someone should wash them soon.

   _____

8. Did someone wash this sweater in hot water?

   _____

9. Luis invited me to the party.

   _____

10. Has anyone invited you to the party?

    _____

► **Practice 16. Review: active vs. passive.** (Charts 10-1 → 10-4)
Make sentences with the given words. Use the present tense. Some are passive and some are not.
Do not change the word order.

1. Sometimes keys \ hide \ under cars

   Sometimes keys are hidden under cars.

2. Cats \ hide \ under cars

   Cats hide under cars.

3. Students \ teach \ by teachers

   _____

4. Students \ study \ a lot

   _____

5. Cereal \ often eat \ at breakfast

   _____

6. Cats \ eat \ cat food

   _____

7. Mice \ eat \ by cats

_____

8. Songs \ sing \ to children \ by their mothers

_____

9. Thai food \ cook \ in Thai restaurants

_____

10. Chefs \ cook \ in restaurants

_____

▶ **Practice 17. Meaning of passive verbs.** (Charts 10-1 → 10-4)
Choose the sentence that has the same meaning as the given sentence.

1. A mouse is being chased.
    a. A mouse is trying to catch something.
    (b.) Something is trying to catch a mouse.

2. The mouse was caught.
    a. The mouse caught something.
    b. Something caught the mouse.

3. The soldiers are being trained.
    a. Someone is training the soldiers.
    b. The soldiers are training someone.

4. The earthquake victims are being helped by the medics.
    a. The medics are receiving help.
    b. The victims are receiving help.

5. Some pets are taught to do tricks.
    a. Some pets teach themselves to do tricks.
    b. Someone teaches the pets to do tricks.

6. The children were trying to find their parents after the school play.
    a. The children were looking for their parents.
    b. The parents were looking for their children.

7. The airline passengers were being asked to wait while the plane was cleaned.
    a. The passengers made a request.
    b. Someone asked the passengers to wait.

8. The flight attendants were instructed to be seated.
    a. Someone told the flight attendants to be seated.
    b. The flight attendants told people to be seated.

▶ **Practice 18. Review: active vs. passive.** (Charts 10-1 → 10-4)
Write "C" if the sentence is correct and "I" if incorrect. Make any necessary corrections.

1. __I__ It ~~was~~ happened many years ago.

2. __C__ Wheat is grown in Canada.

3. _____ I was go to school yesterday.

4. ____ Two firefighters injure while they were fighting the fire.

5. ____ Sara was accidentally broken the window.

6. ____ Kara was eating a snack when the phone rang.

7. ____ Timmy was eaten when the phone rang.

8. ____ I am agree with you.

9. ____ The little boy was fallen down while he was running in the park.

10. ____ The swimmer was died from a shark attack.

11. ____ The swimmer was killed by a shark.

12. ____ I was slept for nine hours last night.

▶ **Practice 19. Passive modals.** (Chart 10-5)
Complete the sentences by changing the active modals to passive modals.

1. This book (*have to return*) _____has to be returned_____ to the library today.

2. That book (*should return*) _____ tomorrow.

3. This letter (*must send*) _____ today.

4. This package (*could send*) _____ tomorrow.

5. That package (*should send*) _____ by overnight mail.

6. That box (*can put away*) _____ now.

7. These boxes (*may throw away*) _____ soon.

8. Those boxes (*might pick up*) _____ this afternoon.

9. This room (*will clean up*) _____ soon.

▶ **Practice 20. Passive modals.** (Chart 10-5)
Change the answers from active to passive. Include the *by*-phrase only if it contains important information.

1. *What happens when an animal is sick?*
   a. A veterinarian should treat the animal.

   _____The animal should be treated by a veterinarian._____

   b. Someone will give the animal medicine.

   _____The animal will be given medicine._____

2. *Can I send this letter now?*
   a. No, someone has to change the last paragraph.

   _____

   b. No, Mr. Hayes must sign it.

   _____

3. *What's going to happen to that big old house on Maple Street?*
   a. A famous hockey star might buy it.

   _____

   b. Someone may convert it into apartments.

   _____

4. *There's a mistake on my credit card bill.*
   a. You should call the credit card company immediately.

   _____

   b. The company ought to fix the mistake right away.

   _____

5. *There's a new book about everyday heroes.*
   a. Everyone should read it.

   _____

   b. They will make a movie of the book.

   _____

6. *This dress is too long for me.*
   a. Someone should shorten it.

   _____

   b. Someone has to do it soon.

   _____

▶ **Practice 21. Summary: active vs. passive.** (Charts 10-1 → 10-5)
Choose the correct verbs.

Telling Time

(1) Sundials (*used* / (*were used*)) in ancient times to tell time. Clocks
first (*appeared* / *were appeared*) during the 13th century. The first watches
(*made* / *were made*) in Europe six hundred years ago. These watches
(*worn* / *were worn*) around a person's neck. In the 1600s, men (*began* / *were begun*)
to put the watches inside their pockets. These watches (*called* / *were called*) pocket
watches. The watches (*became* / *were become*) popular and (*were remained* / *remained*)
popular until World War I. During that war, watches (*put* / *were put*)
on bands, and soldiers (*wore* / *were worn*) the bands around their
wrists. It was more practical to look quickly at a watch on the wrist than to pull a watch out of a
pocket. Since then, millions of wrist watches (*have been manufactured* / *have manufactured*).

(2) However, not as many watches (*are being sold* / *sold*) now as previously. That's because the
time (*is displayed* / *displayed*) by clocks on computers and cell phones. Since computers and cell
phones are everywhere, watches (*aren't needed* / *don't need*) as much as they were. Many young
adults (*have never worn* / *have never been worn*) watches. Some people think that the need for
watches (*may disappear* / *may be disappeared*) completely and that in the future, a wrist watch
(*will be considered* / *will consider*) an antique item, like the pocket watch.

► **Practice 22. Using past participles as adjectives.** (Chart 10-6)
Complete the sentences with the correct prepositions.

Part I. Jack is . . .

1. married ____to____ Katie.

2. excited _____ vacation.

3. exhausted _____ work.

4. frightened _____ heights.

5. disappointed _____ his new car.

6. tired _____ rain.

7. pleased _____ his new boss.

8. involved _____ charity work.

9. worried _____ his elderly parents.

10. acquainted _____ a famous movie star.

Part II. Jack's friend is . . .

11. interested _____ sports.

12. done _____ final exams.

13. terrified _____ spiders.

14. related _____ a famous movie star.

15. opposed _____ private gun ownership.

16. pleased _____ his part-time job.

17. divorced _____ his wife.

Part III. Jack's house is . . .

18. made _____ wood.

19. located _____ the suburbs.

20. crowded _____ antique furniture.

21. prepared _____ emergencies.

► **Practice 23. Using past participles as adjectives.** (Chart 10-6)
Correct the errors.

                    excited about
1. The little girl is ~~excite in~~ her birthday party.

2. Mr. and Mrs. Rose devoted each other.

3. Could you please help me? I need directions. I lost.

4. The students are boring in their chemistry project.

5. The paper bags at this store is composed in recycled products.

6. Your friend needs a doctor. He hurt.

7. How well are you prepare the driver's license test?

8. Mary has been engaging with Paul for five years. Will they ever get married?

▶ **Practice 24. -ed vs. -ing.** (Chart 10-7)
Complete the sentences with the appropriate **-ed** or **-ing** form of the words in parentheses.

Ben is reading a book. He really likes it. He can't put it down. He has to keep reading.

1. The book is really _____interesting_____. (*interest*)

2. Ben is really _____. (*interest*)

3. The story is _____. (*excite*)

4. Ben is _____ about the story. (*excite*)

5. Ben is _____ by the characters in the book. (*fascinate*)

6. The people in the story are _____. (*fascinate*)

7. Ben didn't finish the last book he started because it was _____ and
_____. (*bore, confuse*)

8. Ben doesn't like to read books when he is _____ and
_____. (*bore, confuse*)

9. What is the most _____ book you've read lately? (*interest*)

10. I just finished a _____ mystery story that had a very
_____ ending. (*fascinate, surprise*)

▶ **Practice 25. -ed vs. -ing.** (Chart 10-7)
Choose the correct adjective.

1. The students are (*interesting / interested*) in learning more about Kung Fu.

2. Ms. Green doesn't explain things well. She's (*confusing / confused*). The students are
(*confusing / confused*).

3. Have you heard the news about Jamie and Hal? They are going trekking in Nepal. They are
really (*exciting / excited*) about it. It's really an (*exciting / excited*) thing to do.

4. There was a (*surprising / surprised*) event in the news yesterday: the governor had resigned
suddenly. Everyone was (*surprising / surprised*).

5. It's (*embarrassing* / *embarrassed*) to forget someone's name. Yesterday I couldn't remember the name of my boss's wife, and I felt very (*embarrassed* / *embarrassing*).

6. Mr. Ball fascinates me. He has lived in 13 countries and he speaks five languages. I think he is a (*fascinating* / *fascinated*) person. Whenever I am with him, I listen to everything he says. I am (*fascinating* / *fascinated*) by Mr. Ball.

7. Victor and his wife Sylvia are different. Sylvia is a vegetarian, but Victor isn't. Victor doesn't like Sylvia's cooking. He thinks that the salads she prepares are not (*satisfying* / *satisfied*). He thinks a (*satisfying* / *satisfied*) meal should have plenty of meat.

8. The story of Steven Hawking's life has been (*inspiring* / *inspired*) to many people. Despite terrible handicaps, Steven Hawking became known as a brilliant scientist. I am (*inspiring* / *inspired*) by him.

▶ **Practice 26. -ed vs. -ing.** (Chart 10-7)
Choose the correct adjective.

1. The street signs in our city are (*confused* / (*confusing*)).
2. The drivers are (*frustrated* / *frustrating*).
3. The professor's lecture on anatomy was (*confused* / *confusing*) for the students.
4. Sophie was very (*embarrassed* / *embarrassing*) by all the attention she got for her high test scores.
5. Sophie said it was (*embarrassed* / *embarrassing*) to have so many people congratulate her.
6. I am really (*interested* / *interesting*) in eighteenth-century art.
7. Eighteenth-century art is really (*interested* / *interesting*).
8. What an (*exhausted* / *exhausting*) day! I am so (*tired* / *tiring*) from picking strawberries.
9. Some of the new horror movies are (*frightened* / *frightening*) because they are so realistic.
10. If young children see a horror movie, they often become (*frightened* / *frightening*).

▶ **Practice 27. -ed vs. -ing.** (Chart 10-7)
Write "I" next to the incorrect sentence in each group.

1. a. _____ Science fascinates me.
   b. _____ Science is fascinating to me.
   c. ___*I*___ Science is fascinated to me.

2. a. _____ The baby is exciting about her new toy.
   b. _____ The baby is excited about her new toy.
   c. _____ The new toy is exciting to the baby.

3. a. _____ The book is really interesting.
   b. _____ The book is really interested.
   c. _____ The book interests me.

4. a. _____ I am exhausting from working in the fields.
   b. _____ I am exhausted from working in the fields.
   c. _____ Working in the fields exhausts me.
   d. _____ Working in the fields is exhausting.

5. a. _____ Your grandmother is amazing to me.

   b. _____ Your grandmother amazes me.

   c. _____ Your grandmother is amazed to me.

   d. _____ I am amazed by your grandmother.

► **Practice 28. *Get* + adjective and past participle.** (Chart 10-8)
Choose the correct completion from Column B.

Column A	**Column B**
1. We couldn't go on our vacation to Hawaii because we got _____ with the flu.	a. dressed
2. Jerry couldn't find our house. He got _____ on the way.	b. late
3. Susie is five years old now. She can get _____ by herself.	c. lost
4. When's dinner going to be ready? I'm getting very _____ .	d. arrested
5. We'll be late for the concert if we don't hurry. It's getting _____.	e. wet
6. I want to make a lot of money. Do you know a good way to get _____ quick?	f. rich
7. Jake's in jail now. Yesterday he got _____ for stealing a car.	g. sick
8. Last Saturday we were enjoying our picnic when it suddenly started to rain. We all got _____.	h. hungry

► **Practice 29. *Get* + adjective and past participle.** (Chart 10-8)
Complete the sentences with an appropriate form of ***get***.

1. Hurry up! _____Get_____ busy. There's no time to waste.

2. Tom and Sue _____got_____ married last month.

3. Let's stop working for a while. I _____am getting_____ tired.

4. I _____ interested in biology when I was in high school, so I decided to major

   in it in college.

5. When I was in the hospital, I got a card from my aunt and uncle. It said,

   "_____ well soon."

6. Karen has a new GPS in her car. It tells her exactly how to go everywhere, street by street.

   She used to _____ lost all the time, but she doesn't anymore.

7. A: What happened to you just now?

   B: I don't know. Suddenly I _____ dizzy, but I'm okay now.

8. I always _____ nervous when I have to give a speech.

9. A: Where's Bud? He was supposed to be home two hours ago. He always calls when he's

   late. I _____ worried. Maybe we should call the police.

   B: Relax. He'll be home soon.

10. A: I'm going on a diet.

 B: Oh?

 A: See? This shirt is too tight. I _____ fat.

▶ **Practice 30. Be used/accustomed to.** (Charts 2-8 and 10-9)
Choose the correct completion. More than one answer may be correct.

1. Frank has lived alone for 20 years. He ____ alone.
 a. used to live   (b.) is used to living   (c.) is accustomed to living

2. I ____ with my family, but now I live alone.
 a. used to live   b. am used to living   c. am accustomed to living

3. Rita rides her bike to work every day. She ____ her bike to work.
 a. used to ride   b. is used to riding   c. is accustomed to riding

4. Thomas rode his bike to work for many years, but now he takes the bus. Tom ____ his bike to work.
 a. used to ride   b. is used to riding   c. is accustomed to riding

5. Carl ____ to work, but now he takes a train.
 a. used to drive   b. is used to driving   c. is accustomed to driving

6. Carl drives 50 miles to work every day. He ____ 50 miles a day.
 a. used to drive   b. is used to driving   c. is accustomed to driving

7. Ari ____ dinner at 9:00 P.M. He has dinner at that time every night. That's too late for me.
 a. used to eat   b. is used to eating   c. is accustomed to eating

8. Maria ____ dinner at 9:00 P.M., but now she eats at 6:00 P.M. with her roommates.
 a. used to eat   b. is used to eating   c. is accustomed to eating

▶ **Practice 31. Used to vs. be used to.** (Chart 10-10)
Add an appropriate form of *be* if necessary. If no form of *be* is needed, write Ø.

1. People ___Ø___ used to take trains to travel long distances, but today, most people take airplanes.

2. Polly Hudson often has to travel for her job. She ___is___ used to traveling by plane.

3. You and I are from different cultures. You _____ used to having fish for breakfast. I _____ used to having cheese and bread for breakfast.

4. When I lived at home, I _____ used to have big breakfasts. Now I am living in an apartment on my own, and I don't eat breakfast anymore.

5. Jeremy wakes up at 5:00 every morning for work. After a year of doing this, he _____ used to getting up early, even on weekends.

6. Our neighbor, Dr. Jenkins, retired last year. He _____ used to get up early to go to work at the hospital, but now he gets up whenever he wants.

7. Before email, people _____ used to write letters. Letters are less common nowadays.

8. My grandfather doesn't use the computer much. He _____ used to talking on the phone. When he wants to communicate with us, he phones us.

9. Minna Lee has been our senator for several years. She has never lost an election. She _____ used to winning elections.

10. Sam Sibley _____ used to be our senator. He was our senator for 26 years until he died at age 87.

▶ **Practice 32. *Used to* vs. *be used to*.** (Chart 10-10)
Complete the sentences with *used to* or *be used to* and the correct form of the verb in parentheses.

1. Kate grew up on a farm. She (*get*) _____*used to get*_____ up at dawn and go to bed as soon as the sun went down. Now she works in the city at an advertising agency and has different sleeping hours.

2. Hiroki's workweek is seven days long. He (*work*) _____ on Saturdays and Sundays.

3. Luis spends weekends with his family now. He (*play*) _____ soccer on a team before he was married, but now he enjoys staying home with his young children.

4. Sally (*be*) _____ a nurse. But six years ago, she applied to medical school and was accepted. Now she is a doctor.

5. Joan has taught kindergarten for eight years. She is very patient with small children. She (*work*) _____ with them.

6. Bebo really likes hot and spicy food. He always orders it in a restaurant. He (*eat*) _____ hot and spicy food, and he never orders anything else.

▶ **Practice 33. *Be supposed to*.** (Chart 10-11)
Make sentences with a similar meaning by using a form of *be supposed to*.

1. Someone expected me to return this book to the library yesterday, but I didn't.
   _____*I was supposed to return this book to the library.*_____

2. Our professor expects us to read Chapter 9 before class tomorrow.
   _____

3. Someone expected me to go to a party last night, but I stayed home.
   _____

4. The teacher expects us to do Exercise 10 for homework.
   _____

5. The weather bureau has predicted rain for tomorrow.
   _____

6. The directions on the pill bottle say, "Take one pill every six hours."
   _____

7. My mother expects me to dust the furniture and vacuum the carpet.
   _____

► **Practice 34. Editing.** (Chapter 10)
Correct the errors.

1. The moving boxes _∧ packed by Pierre.
   were

2. My uncle was died in the war.

3. Miami located in Florida.

4. I was very worry about my son.

5. Mr. Rivera interested in finding a new career.

6. Did you tell everyone the shocked news?

7. After ten years, I finally used to this wet and rainy climate.

8. The newspaper suppose to come every morning before eight.

9. The Millers have been marry with each other for 60 years.

10. I am use to drink coffee with cream, but now I drink it black*.

11. What was happen at the party last night?

12. Several people almost get kill when the fireworks exploded over them.

13. A new parking garage being build for our office.

14. I have been living in England for several years, so I accustom driving on the left side of the road.

---

black = without cream.

Change this sentence to the passive:

The fisherman caught six large fish.

There will be eight words in the new passive sentence. Find the words in the puzzle and circle them. The words may be horizontal, vertical, or diagonal. The first letter of each word is highlighted in gray.

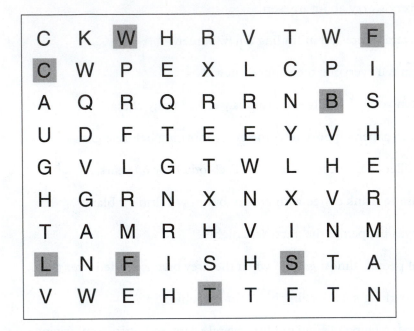

C K W H R V T W F
C W P E X L C P I
A Q R Q R R N B S
U D F T E E Y V H
G V L G T W L H E
H G R N X N X V R
T A M R H V I N M
L N F I S H S T A
V W E H T T F T N

Chapter 11

Count/Noncount Nouns and Articles

▶ **Practice 1. A vs. an: singular count nouns.** (Chart 11-1)
Write **a** or **an**.

1. ___*a*___ game
2. _____ office
3. _____ car
4. _____ egg
5. _____ man
6. _____ university
7. _____ umbrella
8. _____ house
9. _____ island
10. _____ ocean
11. _____ hour

12. _____ horse
13. _____ star
14. _____ eye
15. _____ new game
16. _____ large office
17. _____ old car
18. _____ used car
19. _____ honest man
20. _____ large university
21. _____ small house
22. _____ empty house

▶ **Practice 2. Count and noncount nouns.** (Chart 11-2)
Circle the correct answer.

1. Sal is sitting in (*chair / a chair*).

2. There are four (*chair / chairs*) at the table.

3. There are some (*chair / chairs*) near the wall.

4. One (*chair / chairs*) is broken.

5. I like the (*furniture / furnitures*) in this room.

6. (*Some / A*) furniture in this room came from Italy.

7. (*Furniture / A furniture*) can be expensive.

8. Tomorrow we are going to buy (*one / some*) furniture.

9. Sal needs a new (*desk / desks*).

10. He looked at some (*desk / desks*) last week, but they weren't the right size.

► **Practice 3. Noncount nouns.** (Chart 11-3)
Write the words in their correct categories.

✓apples	bracelets	letters	rings
bananas	chairs	necklaces	sofas
beds	checks	oranges	strawberries
✓bills	earrings	packages	tables

Mail	Fruit	Jewelry	Furniture
bills	apples		

► **Practice 4. More noncount nouns.** (Chart 11-4)
Complete the sentences with words from the list.

fun	gold	help	light	thunder	water

1. Sally drank some _____.

2. It's too dark in here. We need some _____.

3. Listen! Is that _____?

4. These rings are made of _____.

5. I need some _____. Can you please carry this package for me?

6. It was a great party. Everybody had _____.

► **Practice 5. Count and noncount nouns.** (Charts 11-1 → 11-4)
Fill in the blanks with *-s/-es* or Ø if nothing should be added.

1. Would you please pass the salt _____ and pepper _____?

2. It's very cold here and there's been a lot of snow _____. You'll need to bring your warm
   boot _____ and a heavy jacket. And don't forget wool sock _____.

3. Dad made some cookie _____ for the children to have with their milk _____.

4. I wasn't hungry for lunch. I just had some soup _____ and some bread _____ and

   butter _____.

5. Pat slipped on the ice _____ and broke two bone _____ in his foot.

6. There has been rain _____ all week. I'd like to see some sunshine _____ soon.

7. Teachers need patience _____ with their students. The teachers are satisfied when the

   students make progress _____.

▶ **Practice 6. Count and noncount nouns.** (Charts 11-2 and 11-4)
Which of the words can follow **one** and which can follow **some**? Write the correct form for each
noun. If the noun does not have a singular form, write Ø.

		one	**some**
1.	word	*word*	*words*
2.	vocabulary	*Ø*	*vocabulary*
3.	slang	_____	_____
4.	homework	_____	_____
5.	assignment	_____	_____
6.	dress	_____	_____
7.	clothing	_____	_____
8.	family	_____	_____
9.	knowledge	_____	_____
10.	information	_____	_____
11.	fact	_____	_____
12.	luck	_____	_____

▶ **Practice 7. Count and noncount nouns.** (Charts 11-1 → 11-4)
Complete the sentences with **a/an** or **Ø**.

1. Tom lived in __a__ big city for many years. However, three years ago he left the city. It had

   __Ø__ pollution and _____ smog, and he couldn't breathe well. Now he lives in _____ small

   town in the mountains. He breathes _____ clean air and drinks _____ fresh water. He knows

   that it was _____ good idea to leave the city because his health is better.

2. Cornell University is named for Ezra Cornell. Ezra Cornell was a philanthropist* who lived in

   Ithaca, New York. He loved the area and wanted to improve it. People there didn't have _____

   library, and so he built one for them. Then, he wanted to build _____ university where people

   could gain _____ knowledge in _____ practical subjects, such as farming, as well as in _____

   history, _____ literature, and _____ science. Cornell owned _____ large farm in the area, and in

   an act of generosity, he donated it as the site for the new university. Cornell University opened

   in 1865, and today it is known as _____ excellent university — one of the best universities in

   the world.

---

philanthropist = a rich person who gives a lot of money to help poor people or good causes.

► **Practice 8. Count and noncount nouns.** (Charts 11-2 → 11-4)
Complete the sentences with words from the list. Use the plural form as necessary.

apple tree	grass	machine	rice
bracelet	jewel	machinery	ring
✓bread	jewelry	mountain	scenery
corn	lake	pea	tool
equipment			

1. I went to the grocery store and bought some _____ *bread,* _____

_____

2. I stood on a hill in the countryside and saw some _____

_____

3. I went to a jewelry store and saw some _____

_____

4. At the auto repair shop, I saw some _____

_____

► **Practice 9. Count and noncount nouns.** (Charts 11-2 → 11-5)
Complete the sentences with *one*, *much*, or *many*.

Do you have . . .

1. _____*one*_____ chair?	9. _____ child?
2. _____*much*_____ furniture?	10. _____ money?
3. _____*many*_____ vegetables?	11. _____ facts?
4. _____ fruit?	12. _____ information?
5. _____ water?	13. _____ stuff?
6. _____ sand?	14. _____ thing?
7. _____ clothing?	15. _____ things?
8. _____ clothes?	16. _____ problems?

► **Practice 10. *Many* vs. *much*.** (Chart 11-5)
Complete the sentences with the correct words from the list. Use the plural form of the noun where necessary.

1. *apple, coffee, fruit, sugar, vegetable*

   a. I didn't buy many _____*apples*_____ or _____.

   b. I didn't buy much _____*coffee*_____, _____, or _____.

2. *English, answer, person, slang, thing*

   a. Mr. Wade doesn't know many _____, _____ and _____.

   b. Mr. Wade doesn't know much _____ or _____.

3. *homework, idea, information, suggestion, work*

   a. Does Sue have many _____ or _____?

   b. Does Sue have much _____, _____ or _____?

4. *crime, garbage, police officer, traffic, violence*

    a. Does this city have many _____.

    b. Does this city have much _____, _____, _____, or _____.

▶ **Practice 11. *How many* and *how much*.** (Chart 11-5)
Complete the questions with *many* or *much*. Add final *-s/-es* if necessary to make a noun plural. (Some of the count nouns have irregular plural forms.) If a verb is needed, circle the correct one in the parentheses. If final *-s/-es* is not necessary, write **Ø**.

1. How _____*many*_____ **letter** _*s*_ (*is* / *(are)*) there in the English alphabet?*

2. How _____*much*_____ **mail** _*Ø*_ did you get yesterday?

3. How _____*many*_____ **man** _*men*_ (*has* / *(have)*) a full beard at least once in their life?

4. How _____ English **literature** _____ have you studied?

5. How _____ English **word** _____ do you know?

6. How _____ **gasoline** _____ does it take to fill the tank in your car?

7. (*British:* How _____ **petrol** _____ does it take to fill the tank?)

8. How _____ **grandchild** _____ does Mrs. Cunningham have?

9. How _____ **fun** _____ did you have at the amusement park?

10. How _____ **island** _____ (*is* / *are*) there in Indonesia?**

11. How _____ **people** _____ will there be by the year 2050?***

12. How _____ **zero** _____ (*is* / *are*) there in a billion?****

▶ **Practice 12. Review: count and noncount nouns.** (Charts 11-1 → 11-5)
Choose all the words that can be used with each given noun.

1. flower	(a)	an	some	much	many
2. flowers	a	an	(some)	much	(many)
3. coin	a	an	some	much	many
4. money	a	an	some	much	many
5. coins	a	an	some	much	many
6. salt	a	an	some	much	many
7. error	a	an	some	much	many
8. mistake	a	an	some	much	many
9. honest mistake	a	an	some	much	many
10. mistakes	a	an	some	much	many
11. dream	a	an	some	much	many
12. interesting dream	a	an	some	much	many
13. questions	a	an	some	much	many

---

*There are twenty-six (26) letters, in the English alphabet.

**More than thirteen thousand seven hundred (13,700).

***Estimated at more than thirteen billion (13,000,000,000).

****Nine (9)

		a	an	some	much	many
14.	soap	a	an	some	much	many
15.	bar of soap	a	an	some	much	many
16.	beauty	a	an	some	much	many
17.	cup of tea	a	an	some	much	many
18.	unsafe place	a	an	some	much	many
19.	fruit	a	an	some	much	many
20.	pieces of fruit	a	an	some	much	many

▶ **Practice 13. A few vs. a little.** (Chart 11-5)
Complete the sentences with **a few** or **a little**. Add a final **-s/-es/-ies** to the noun if necessary. Otherwise, write **Ø**.

1. Everyone needs _____*a little*_____ **help** _*Ø*_ sometimes.

2. The children's native language is Spanish, but they speak _____ **English** _____.

3. We bought _____ **orange** _____ to make fresh orange juice.

4. I like _____ **sugar** _____ in my coffee.

5. I'm going to give you _____ **advice** _____.

6. I need _____ **suggestion** _____.

7. He asked _____ **question** _____.

8. We talked to _____ **people** _____ on the plane.

9. Please give me _____ more **minute** _____.

10. I have _____ **work** _____ to do over the weekend.

11. Pedro already knew _____ English **grammar** _____ before he took this English course.

12. I've been making _____ **progress** _____ in the last couple of weeks.

▶ **Practice 14. Count and noncount nouns: summary.** (Chart 11-5)
Draw a line through the expressions of quantity that <u>cannot</u> be used to complete the sentences.

1. I get ____ mail every day.
   a. a lot of
   b. some
   c. a little
   d. ~~a few~~
   e. too much
   f. too many
   g. several
   h. three

2. I get ____ letters every day.
   a. a lot of
   b. some
   c. a little
   d. a few
   e. too much
   f. too many
   g. several
   h. three

3. I ate _____ fruit.

   a. some

   b. a little

   c. a few

   d. too many

   e. too much

4. I ate _____ apples.

   a. several

   b. many

   c. too much

   d. some

   e. a lot of

5. There is _____ traffic in the street.

   a. several

   b. some

   c. too many

   d. a little

   e. a lot of

   f. a few

   g. too much

   h. five

6. There are _____ cars in the street.

   a. several

   b. some

   c. too many

   d. a little

   e. a lot of

   f. a few

   g. too much

   h. five

▶ **Practice 15. Count and noncount nouns.** (Charts 6-2 and 11-1 → 11-6)
Add **-s** where necessary.

Plants

(1) Scientist _____ divide living things into two groups: animal _____ and plant _____. Animals move around from one place _____ to another, but plants don't. Plants stay in one place.

(2) Many plants, such as flower _____, grass, and tree _____, grow on land. Some plants grow only in desert _____ and some grow only in ocean _____. There are a few plants that grow on the tops of mountain _____ and even in the polar regions.

(3) Plants that people grow for food are called crops. Rice _____ is a crop _____ that grows in many parts of the world _____. Other common crops include potatoes, wheat, and corn. All crop _____ depend on nature. Bad weather _____, such as too much or too little rain, can destroy wheat or corn field _____.

(4) Plant _____ are also important to our health _____. We get a lot of medicines from plants. In addition, plants clean the air _____. Many tree _____ and other plants remove bad gasses from the atmosphere and release oxygen into the air. The more plants we have on earth _____, the healthier the air _____ is.

► **Practice 16. Nouns that can be count or noncount.** (Chart 11-6)
Complete the sentences with the correct word from Column B.

Column A

1. We have been to Italy several _____.
2. I don't like beef, but I do like _____.
3. On the table there were plates, forks, knives, and _____.
4. Drivers should turn on their _____ before it gets dark.
5. Please open the curtains. There's not enough _____ in this room.
6. Rosa is 40. She has a few gray _____.
7. A fish bowl is made of _____.
8. My grandparents have a small farm with about 50 _____.
9. Al is getting bald. He is losing his _____.
10. I couldn't finish the exam. There wasn't enough _____.

Column B

a. chicken
b. glass
c. hair
d. time
e. times
f. chickens
g. glasses
h. hairs
i. lights
j. light

► **Practice 17. Units of measure with noncount nouns.** (Chart 11-7)
What units of measure are usually used with the following nouns? More than one unit of measure can be used with some of the nouns.

| bag | bottle | box | can / tin* | jar |

1. a _____jar_____ of pickles.
2. a _____ of aspirin.
3. a _____ of laundry detergent
4. a _____ of instant coffee
5. a _____ of sardines
6. a _____ of sugar
7. a _____ of peanut butter
8. a _____ of soy sauce
9. a _____ of uncooked noodles
10. a _____ of beans

► **Practice 18. Units of measure with noncount nouns.** (Chart 11-7)
Complete the sentences with words from the list. Use the plural form if necessary. Some sentences have more than one possible completion.

| bottle | ✓cup | glass | loaf | pound |
| carton | gallon | kilo | piece | sheet |

1. I drank a _____cup_____ of coffee.
2. I bought two _____pounds/kilos_____ of flour.

_____

*a can = a tin in British English

3. I drank a _____ of orange juice.

4. I put ten _____ of gas in my car.

5. I bought a _____ of milk at the supermarket.

6. I need a _____ of chalk.

7. I used two _____ of bread to make a sandwich.

8. There is a _____ of fruit on the table.

9. There are 200 _____ of lined paper in my notebook.

10. I bought one _____ of bread at the store.

11. Let me give you a _____ of advice.

12. I just learned an interesting _____ of information.

▶ **Practice 19. Much vs. many.** (Charts 11-5 → 11-7)
Complete the questions with *much* or *many* and the appropriate noun.

Going on a Trip

1. A: Are you all packed for your trip to Tahiti? How _____*many suitcases*_____ are you taking with you?
   B: Three. (I'm taking three suitcases.)

2. A: How _____*much sunscreen*_____ are you taking?
   B: A lot. (I'm taking a lot of sunscreen.)

3. A: How _____ are you taking?
   B: Two pairs. (I'm taking two pairs of sandals.)

4. A: How _____ did you pack?
   B: One tube. (I packed one tube of toothpaste.)

5. A: How _____ will you and Sandy have?
   B: I'm not sure. Maybe 20 kilos. (We may have 20 kilos of luggage.)

6. A: How _____ will you pay in overweight baggage charges?
   B: A lot. (We will pay of lot of money for overweight baggage.)

7. A: How _____ will you be away?
   B: Twelve. (We'll be away for twelve days.)

▶ **Practice 20. A/an vs. some.** (Chart 11-8)
Complete the sentences with *a/an* or *some*.

1. I wrote ____*a*____ **letter**.

2. I got ____*some*____ **mail**.

3. We bought _____ **equipment** for our camping trip.

4. You need _____ **tool** to cut wood.

5. I wore _____ old **clothing**.

6. I wore _____ old **shirt**.

7. Jim asked me for _____ **advice**.

8. I gave Jim _____ **suggestion**.

9. I gave Jim _____ **suggestions**.

10. I read _____ interesting **story** in the paper.

11. The paper has _____ interesting **news** today.

12. I know _____ **song** from India.

13. I know _____ Indian **music**.

14. I learned _____ new **word**.

15. I learned _____ new **slang**.

▶ **Practice 21. A/an vs. some.** (Chart 11-8)
Complete the sentences with *a/an* or *some*.

1. A: What did you do this morning?
   B: I woke up early. I ate a big breakfast. I had ____*a*____ glass of fresh orange juice, _____ eggs, _____ piece of toast with _____ butter, and _____ delicious coffee.

2. A: What did you do this afternoon?
   B: I went to the store. I bought _____ sugar, _____ flour, and _____ milk to make dessert for my grandma's birthday tonight. We'll have it with _____ vanilla ice cream.

3. A: What did you do last weekend?
   B: We went bird watching. We saw _____ beautiful birds and we heard _____ bird songs. We heard _____ bird that was singing _____ song very loudly. Soon another bird was singing. Then many birds began to sing at the same time. They made _____ lovely music.

▶ **Practice 22. A/an vs. the: singular count nouns.** (Chart 11-8)
Complete the sentences with *a/an* or *the*.

1. A: ____*A*____ dog makes a good pet.
   B: I agree.

2. A: Did you feed ___*the*___ dog?
   B: Yes, I did.

3. My dorm room has _____ desk, _____ bed, _____ chest of drawers, and two chairs.

4. A: Jessica, where's the stapler?
   B: On _____ desk. If it's not there, look in _____ top drawer.

5. A: Sara, put your bike in _____ garage before dark.
   B: Okay, Dad.

6. Our house has _____ garage. We keep our car and our bikes there.

7. Almost every sentence has _____ subject and _____ verb.

8. Look at this sentence: *Luca lives in Miami.* What is _____ subject, and what is _____ verb?

9. A: I can't see you at four. I'll be in _____ meeting then. How about four-thirty?
   B: Fine.

10. A: What time does _____ meeting start Tuesday?
    B: Eight o'clock.

11. Max's car ran out of gas. He didn't have cell phone reception, so he had to walk _____

    long distance to find _____ telephone and call his brother for help.

12. _____ distance from _____ sun to _____ earth is 93,000,000 miles.

13. A: Where do you live?
    B: We live on _____ quiet street in the suburbs.

14. A: Is this _____ street where Jamie lives?
    B: Yes, it is.

► **Practice 23. Using *the* for second mention.** (Charts 11-6 → 11-8)
Complete the sentences with *a/an, some,* or *the*. Note: Use *the* when a noun is mentioned for the second time.

1. I had _____ soup and _____ sandwich for lunch. _____ soup was too salty, but

   _____ sandwich was pretty good.

2. Yesterday I bought _____ clothes. I bought _____ suit, _____ shirt, and

   _____ tie. _____ suit is gray and comes with a vest. _____ shirt is pale blue, and

   _____ tie has black and gray stripes.

3. A: I saw _____ accident yesterday.

   B: Oh? Where?

   A: On Grand Avenue. _____ man in _____ Volkswagen drove through a stop sign

      and hit _____ bus.

   B: Was anyone hurt in _____ accident?

   A: I don't think so. _____ man who was driving _____ Volkswagen got out of his car
      and seemed to be okay. His car was only slightly damaged. No one on _____ bus was
      hurt.

4. Yesterday I saw _____ man and _____ woman. They were having _____

   argument. _____ man was yelling at _____ woman, and _____ woman was

   shouting at _____ man. I don't know what _____ argument was about.

► **Practice 24. Using *the* for second mention.** (Charts 11-6 → 11-8)
Complete the sentences with *a/an, some,* or *the*.

One day last month while I was driving through the countryside, I saw ___*a*___ man and
                                                                           1

_____ truck next to _____ covered bridge. _____ bridge crossed _____ small
   2   3   4   5

river. I stopped and asked _____ man, "What's the matter? Can I help?"
                              6

"Well," said _____ man, "My truck is about a half-inch* too tall. Or maybe _____ top
                    7   8
of _____ bridge is a half-inch too short. Either way, my truck won't fit under _____
         9   10
bridge."

"Hmmm. There must be _____ solution to this problem," I said.
                              11

"I don't know. I guess I'll have to turn around and take another route," he replied.

After a few moments of thought, I said, "I have _____ solution!"
                                                        12

"What is it?" asked the man.

"Let a little air out of your tires. Then _____ truck won't be too tall, and you can cross
                                                 13

_____ bridge over _____ river."
      14   15

"Hey, that's _____ great idea. Let's try it!" So _____ man let a little air out of
                   16   17

_____ tires and was able to cross _____ river and go on his way.
      18   19

▶ **Practice 25. Summary: _a/an_ vs. _the_ vs. Ø.** (Chart 11-8)
Complete the sentences with **_a/an, the_**, or **Ø**. Add capital letters as necessary.

1. It is _____ scientific fact: _____ steam rises when _____ water boils.

2. _____ gas is expensive nowadays.

3. _____ gas I got yesterday cost more than I've ever paid.

4. _____ sun is _____ star. We need _____ sun for _____ heat, _____
   light, and _____ energy.

5. A: Do you see _____ man who is standing next to Janet?
   B: Yes. Who is he?

   A: He's _____ president of this university.

6. A one-dollar bill has a picture of _____ president of the United States. It's a picture of
   George Washington. He was _____ first president of the country.

---

*One-half inch = 1.27 centimeters

7. _____ pizza originated in Italy. It is a pie with _____ cheese, _____ tomatoes, and other things on top.

PIZZA

CHEESE AND ONION... MUSHROOM AND CHEESE...
PEPPERONI.... PINEAPPLE AND CANADIAN BACON...
SAUSAGE....
VEGETARIAN...

8. A: Hey, Nick. Pass _____ pizza. I want another piece.
   B: There are only two pieces left. You take _____ big piece, and I'll take _____ small one.

9. I had _____ interesting experience yesterday. _____ man in _____ blue suit came into my office and handed me _____ bouquet of _____ flowers. I had never seen _____ man before in my life, but I thanked him for _____ flowers. Then he walked out _____ door.

▶ **Practice 26. Using _the_ or Ø with names.** (Chart 11-9)
Complete the sentences with **_the_** or **Ø**.

1. Although Ingrid has been in Orly Airport several times, she has never visited ___Ø___ Paris.

2. ___Ø___ Dr. James was the youngest person at her university to get a Ph.D.

3. _____ Mount Rainier in Washington state is in _____ Cascade Mountain Range.

4. _____ Nile is the longest river in _____ Africa.

5. Is _____ Toronto or _____ Montreal the largest city in Canada?

6. During her tour of Africa, Helen climbed _____ Mount Kilimanjaro and visited several national parks in _____ Kenya.

7. _____ New Zealand is made up of two islands: North Island and South Island.

8. _____ Himalayas extend through several countries, including Pakistan, _____ India, and _____ Nepal.

9. _____ President Davis was surprised to be elected to a fourth term.

10. _____ Ho Chi Minh City in _____ Vietnam was formerly called _____ Saigon.

11. _____ Andes Mountains in South America extend for 5000 miles.

12. _____ Dominician Republic and _____ Haiti share an island called Hispaniola. _____ Atlantic Ocean is at the north, and _____ Caribbean Sea is at the south.

► **Practice 27. Using *the* or Ø with names.** (Chart 11-9)
Answer the questions. Choose from the list below. Use *the* if necessary. (Not all names on the list will be used.)

Africa	Europe	Mont Blanc	Saudi Arabia
Alps	Gobi Desert	Mount Vesuvius	Shanghai
Amazon River	Indian Ocean	Netherlands	South America
Beijing	Lagos	Nepal	Taipei
Black Sea	Lake Baikal	Nile River	Thames River
✓Dead Sea	Lake Tanganyika	North America	United Arab Emirates
Elbe River	Lake Titicaca	Sahara Desert	Urals

Geography Trivia

Question	Answer
1. What is the lowest point on earth?	*the Dead Sea*
2. What is the second-longest river in the world?	_____
3. What is the most populated city in China?	_____
4. What is the largest desert in the world?	_____
5. What river runs through London?	_____
6. On what continent is the Volga River?	_____
7. What mountains border France and Italy?	_____
8. What lake is in east central Africa?	_____
9. On what continent is Mexico?	_____
10. What is the third-largest ocean in the world?	_____
11. What country is also known as Holland?	_____
12. What is the third-largest continent in the world?	_____
13. What country is located in the Himalayas?	_____
14. What mountains are part of the boundary between Europe and Asia?	_____
15. What is the capital of Nigeria?	_____
16. What country consists of seven kingdoms?	_____

► **Practice 28. Capitalization.** (Chart 11-10)
Add capital letters where necessary.

1. I'm taking ᴮɓiology 101 this semester.

2. I'm taking history, biology, english, and calculus this semester.

3. Some lab classes meet on saturday.

4. My roommate likes vietnamese food, and i like thai food.

5. Shelia works for the xerox corporation. it is a very large corporation.

6. Pedro is from latin america. He speaks spanish.

7. My favorite park is central park in new york.

8. Do you know my uncle?

9. I like uncle joe and aunt sara.

10. susan w. miller is a professor.

11. I am in prof. miller's class.

12. In january, it's winter in canada and summer in argentina.

13. I would like to visit los angeles.

14. It's the largest city in california.

▶ **Practice 29. Editing.** (Chapter 11)
Correct the errors.

                                           letter
1. The mail carrier brought only one ~~mail~~ today.

2. Mr. Dale gave his class long history assignment for the weekend.

3. Tariq speaks several language, including Arabic and German.

4. I usually have glass water with my lunch.

5. A helpful police officer gave us an information about the city.

6. This recipe calls for two cup of nut.

7. Much vegetable are believed to have cancer-fighting ingredients.

8. Only applicants with the necessary experiences should apply for the computer position.

9. When Vicki likes a movie, she sees it several time.

10. A popular children's story is *Snow White and the Seven Dwarfs.*

11. Is it possible to stop all violences in the world?

12. Some of the homeworks for my English class was easy, but many of the assignment were unclear.

13. Diane has been to Rome several time recently. She always has wonderful time.

14. Many parents need advices about raising children.

15. A person doesn't need many equipment to play baseball: just ball and a bat.

Complete the puzzle. Use the clues to find the correct words. All the words are from Chapter 11.

Across

1. There isn't much _____ from the earthquake area. All the communication lines are down, and we can't get any news.

8. Our teacher gave us some good _____ to find helpful websites.

9. Please hurry. We don't have much _____.

10. There are too _____ cars on the road.

Down

2. I wanted to buy some candy, so my grandfather gave me a _____ dollars.

3. The doctor gave me some good _____: Exercise regularly.

4. I have seen this movie four _____.

5. My grandmother handed me a _____ money — about 10 dollars.

6. You don't need _____ equipment to play tennis: just a tennis racket and some tennis balls.

7. I was afraid to hear the truth, but now I am glad you told me everything. I appreciate your _____.

Chapter 12
Adjective Clauses

▶ **Practice 1. Using *who* and *that* in adjective clauses to describe people.**
(Charts 12-1 and 12-2)

<u>Underline</u> the adjective clause in the long sentence. Then change the long sentence into two short sentences.*

1. *Long sentence:*   I thanked the man <u>who helped me move the refrigerator</u>.

   Short sentence 1: _____ I thanked _____ the man.

   Short sentence 2: _____ He helped _____ me move the refrigerator.

2. *Long sentence:*   A woman who was wearing a gray suit asked me for directions.

   Short sentence 1: _____ me for directions.

   Short sentence 2: _____ a gray suit.

3. *Long sentence:*   I saw a man that was wearing a blue coat.

   Short sentence 1: _____ a man.

   Short sentence 2: _____ a blue coat.

4. *Long sentence:*   The parents hugged the boy who had pulled his brother from the icy river.

   Short sentence 1: _____ the boy.

   Short sentence 2: _____ his brother from the icy river.

5. *Long sentence:*   The girl that broke the vase apologized to Mrs. Cook.

   Short sentence 1: _____ to Mrs. Cook.

   Short sentence 2: _____ the vase.

---

*In grammar terminology, the "long sentence" is called a **complex sentence**, and the "short sentence" is called a **simple sentence**.

- A complex sentence has an independent clause and one or more dependent clauses. For example:
  I thanked the man who helped me. = a complex sentence consisting of one independent clause (*I thanked the man*) and one dependent clause (*who helped me*)
- A simple sentence has only an independent clause. For example:
  I thanked the man. = a simple sentence consisting of one independent clause
  He helped me. = a simple sentence consisting of one independent clause

▶ **Practice 2. Using *who* and *that* in adjective clauses to describe people.**
(Chart 12-2)
Underline each adjective clause. Then write "S" above its subject, and "V" above its verb.

                    S   V

1. The people <u>who live next to me</u> are nice.

2. My neighbors who live across the street have a new baby.

3. A family that is from India just moved to our street.

4. Our neighborhood is a good place for people who have children.

5. A professor who teaches at the university just moved to our street.

6. One of my neighbors has a disabled child who is training to play basketball in the Special Olympics.

▶ **Practice 3. Using *who* and *that* in adjective clauses to describe people.**
(Chart 12-2)
Combine the two short sentences into one long sentence using "short sentence 2" as an adjective clause. Write two sentences: the first with ***who*** and the second with ***that***.

1. *Short sentence 1:*   The woman was polite.

   Short sentence 2:   She answered the phone.

   Long sentence 1:   The woman _____*who answered the phone*_____ was polite.

   Long sentence 2:   The woman _____*that answered the phone*_____ was polite.

2. *Short sentence 1:*   The man is also a singer.

   Short sentence 2:   The man played the guitar.

   Long sentence 1:   The man _____ is also a singer.

   Long sentence 2:   The man _____ is also a singer.

3. *Short sentence 1:*   I read about the soccer player.

   Short sentence 2:   He was injured yesterday.

   Long sentence 1:   I read about the soccer player _____ yesterday.

   Long sentence 2:   I read about the soccer player _____ yesterday.

4. *Short sentence 1:*   I know a man.

   Short sentence 2:   He has sailed around the world.

   Long sentence 1:   I know a man _____ around the world.

   Long sentence 2:   I know a man _____ around the world.

▶ **Practice 4. Using *who* and *that* in adjective clauses to describe people.**
(Chart 12-2)
Complete the sentences using either **who** or **that**.

1. A hair cutter is a person _____ *who / that cuts hair* _____.

2. A pizza maker is a person _____.

3. A tennis player is a person _____.

4. An English teacher is a person _____.

5. A horse trainer is a person _____.

6. A meat eater is a person _____.

7. Tea drinkers are people _____.

8. Firefighters are people _____.

▶ **Practice 5. Using *who, whom, that,* and *Ø* in adjective clauses.** (Chart 12-3)
Change the two short sentences into one long sentence as indicated. <u>Underline</u> the adjective clause.

1. *Short sentence 1:*   The woman was polite.
   Short sentence 2:   Jack met her.

   Long sentence with **that**:   The woman _____ *that Jack met* _____ was polite.

2. *Short sentence 1:*   The woman was very tall.
   Short sentence 2:   Jack saw her.

   Long sentence with **Ø**:   The woman _____ was very tall.

3. *Short sentence 1:*   The woman is a professor.
   Short sentence 2:   Jack knows her.

   Long sentence with **that**:   The woman _____ is a professor.

4. *Short sentence 1:*   The student was grateful.
   Short sentence 2:   The teacher helped the student.

   Long sentence with **that**:   The student _____ was grateful.

5. *Short sentence 1:*   The student was happy about the exam.
   Short sentence 2:   I helped the student.

   Long sentence with **Ø**:   The student _____ was happy
   about the exam.

6. *Short sentence 1:*   The student won a scholarship.
   Short sentence 2:   I just met the student.

   Long sentence with **who**:   The student _____ won a
   scholarship.

7. *Short sentence 1:*   The student is the class president.
    Short sentence 2:   You see the student over there.

    Long sentence with **whom**:   The student _____ is the class president.

▶ **Practice 6. Using *who* and *that* in adjective clauses.** (Charts 12-2 and 12-3)
Write "S" if **who** or **that** is the subject of the adjective clause. Write "O" if **who** or **that** is the object of the adjective clause. Cross out the words **who** or **that** where possible.

1. __S__ The students **who** go to this school are friendly.
2. __O__ The people ~~that~~ I saw in the park were practicing yoga.
3. ____ I saw several people **who** were practicing yoga.
4. ____ I know the woman **that** my uncle hired.
5. ____ I like the woman **that** manages my uncle's store.
6. ____ Do you like the mechanic **that** fixed your car?
7. ____ Mr. Polanski is a mechanic **who** you can trust.
8. ____ What's the name of the woman **who** Hank invited to the dance?
9. ____ Do you know the man **who**'s dancing with Katrina?
10. ____ The singer **that** we just heard comes from Mexico.
11. ____ The singer **who** just performed comes from Mexico.

▶ **Practice 7. Using *who, whom, that,* and *Ø* in adjective clauses.** (Chart 12-3)
Circle all the correct completions.

1. A man ____ works on a submarine.
    a. I know
    b. whom I know
    c. who I know
    d. that I know

2. I know a man ____ on a submarine.
    a. works
    b. he works
    c. who works
    d. that works

3. My mother is a woman ____ tremendously.
    a. I admire
    b. whom I admire
    c. who I admire
    d. that I admire

4. My mother is a woman ____
    a. is always optimistic
    b. she is always optimistic
    c. who is always optimistic
    d. that is always optimistic

5. I'm pleased with the person ____.
    a. he is going to be our next mayor
    b. who is going to be our next mayor
    c. whom is going to be our next mayor
    d. that is going to be our next mayor

6. I'm pleased with the person ____.
    a. the people elected
    b. that the people elected
    c. who the people elected
    d. the people elected him

▶ **Practice 8. Using *that, who, whom* and Ø in adjective clauses.** (Chart 12-3)
In the box, write every possible pronoun that can be used to connect the adjective clause to the main clause: *who, that,* or *whom*. Also, write Ø if the pronoun can be omitted.

1. The woman | who / that | sat next to me on the plane was very friendly.

2. The woman | that / Ø / who / whom | I met on the plane was very friendly.

3. Two people | | I didn't know walked into the classroom.

4. The people | | walked into the classroom were strangers.

5. My cousin's wife is the woman | | is talking to Mr. Horn.

6. I like the woman | | my brother and I met on the bus.

▶ **Practice 9. *Who* vs. *which*.** (Charts 12-2 → 12-4)
Choose the correct completion.

1. The magazine _____ I read on the plane was interesting.
   a. who   (b.) which

2. The artist _____ drew my picture is very good.
   a. who   b. which

3. I really enjoyed the experiences _____ I had on my trip to Nigeria.
   a. who   b. which

4. Most of the games _____ we played as children no longer entertain us.
   a. who   b. which

5. All of the people _____ I called yesterday can come to the meeting on Monday.
   a. who   b. which

6. The teacher _____ was ill canceled her math class.
   a. who   b. which

7. The flight _____ I took to Singapore was on time.
   a. who   b. which

8. I read an article _____ discussed the current political crisis.
   a. who   b. which

▶ **Practice 10. *That* and *which*.** (Chart 12-4)
Write "S" if *that* or *which* is the subject of the adjective clause. Write "O" if *that* or *which* is the object of the adjective clause. Cross out the words *that* or *which* where possible.

1. __O__ The medicine ~~which~~ the doctor prescribed for me was very expensive.

2. __S__ The medicine **which** is on the shelf is no longer good.

3. _____ The computer **that** I bought recently has already crashed several times.

4. _____ The car **which** my husband drives is very reliable.

5. _____ The house **which** sits on top of the hill has won several architecture awards.

6. _____ The restaurant **that** offered low-cost dinners to senior citizens has recently closed.

7. _____ The trees **that** shade our house are over 300 years old.

8. _____ The trees **that** we planted last year have doubled in size.

▶ **Practice 11. Using *that*, *which*, and Ø in adjective clauses.** (Chart 12-4)
Write the pronouns *which* or *that* that can be used to connect the adjective clause to the main clause. Also write Ø if the pronoun can be omitted.

1. I really enjoyed the movie │ *that* / *which* / Ø │ we saw last night.

2. Tim liked the movie [ ] was playing at the Fox Theater.

3. The plane [ ] I took to Korea was two hours late because of bad weather.

4. The books [ ] Jane ordered came in the mail today.

5. Jane was glad to get the books [ ] came in the mail today.

► **Practice 12. Adjective clauses.** (Charts 12-3 and 12-4)
Complete the sentences with adjective clauses using words from the lists. There is one extra word in each list.

1. *them, I, visited*

   I enjoy the relatives _____<u>I visited</u>_____ in Mexico City last year.

2. *I, that, drank, it*

   The coffee _____ was cold and weak.

3. *wearing, was, I, them*

   The tennis shoes _____ in the garden got wet and muddy.

4. *that, him, I've, known, and, loved*

   My cousin Ahmed is a person _____ since he was born.

5. *her, I, married, who*

   I have a great deal of respect for the wonderful woman _____ 11 years ago.

6. *have, had, him, we, that*

   The dog _____ for several years is very gentle with young children.

7. *which, it, we, bought*

   The car _____ last year has turned out to be a lemon.*

► **Practice 13. Pronoun usage in adjective clauses.** (Charts 12 → 12-4)
Choose <u>all</u> the correct answers.

1. I liked the teacher _____ I had for chemistry in high school.
   (a.) who   (b.) whom   c. which   (d.) that   (e.) Ø

2. I liked chemistry because the teacher _____ taught the class was excellent.
   a. who   b. whom   c. which   d. that   e. Ø

3. The researchers in the Amazon River basin found many plants _____ were previously unknown.
   a. who   b. whom   c. which   d. that   e. Ø

4. The plants _____ the researchers found were carefully taken to a laboratory.
   a. who   b. whom   c. which   d. that   e. Ø

5. Mr. Rice made sandwiches for the children _____ were hungry.
   a. who   b. whom   c. which   d. that   e. Ø

6. The children enjoyed the sandwiches _____ Mr. Rice made for them.
   a. who   b. whom   c. which   d. that   e. Ø

7. Have you read any books by the author _____ the teacher mentioned in class?
   a. who   b. whom   c. which   d. that   e. Ø

---

*lemon = something, especially a car, that doesn't work properly and needs a lot of repairs.

8. A book _____ I read last year has become a best-seller.

    a. who   b. whom   c. which   d. that   e. Ø

9. The fans _____ were sitting in the stadium jumped up and cheered when their team scored a point.

    a. who   b. whom   c. which   d. that   e. Ø

10. The fans jumped up and cheered when their team scored the point _____ won the game.

    a. who   b. whom   c. which   d. that   e. Ø

▶ **Practice 14. Singular and plural verbs in adjective clauses.** (Chart 12-5)
Choose the correct form of the verb in *italics*. <u>Underline</u> the noun that determines whether the verb in the adjective clause is singular or plural.

1. The <u>students</u> who (*is* / (*are*)) in my class come from many countries.

2. The people who (*is* / *are*) standing in line to get into the theater have been here for a couple of hours.

3. Water is a chemical compound that (*consists* / *consist*) of oxygen and hydrogen.

4. There are two students in my class who (*speaks* / *speak*) Portuguese.

5. I met some people who (*knows* / *know*) my brother.

6. The student who (*is* / *are*) talking to the teacher is from Peru.

7. Do you know the people that (*lives* / *live*) in that house?

8. A carpenter is a person who (*makes* / *make*) things out of wood.

9. Sculptors are artists who (*make* / *makes*) things from clay or other materials.

▶ **Practice 15. Prepositions in adjective clauses.** (Chart 12-6 and Appendix 2)
Complete the sentences with adjective clauses. Add prepositions as necessary.

1. We went to a movie. The movie was good.

   a. The movie that _____<u>we went to</u>_____ was good.

   b. The movie Ø _____<u>we went to</u>_____ was good.

2. I enjoyed meeting the people yesterday. You introduced me to them.

   a. I enjoyed meeting the people that _____ yesterday.

   b. I enjoyed meeting the people who _____ yesterday.

3. English grammar is a subject. I am quite familiar with English grammar.

   a. English grammar is a subject Ø _____.

   b. English grammar is a subject with _____.

4. Ms. Perez can help you. You should talk with her.

   a. Ms. Perez is the person Ø _____.

   b. Ms. Perez is the person with _____.

5. The train is usually late. We are waiting for it.

   a. The train that _____ is usually late.

   b. The train Ø _____ is usually late.

6. The job requires several years of experience. I'm interested in the job.

   a. The job that _____ requires several years of experience.

   b. The job which _____ requires several years of experience.

▶ **Practice 16. Prepositions in adjective clauses.** (Chart 12-6)
Give all the possible patterns for the adjective clause: *that, which, who, whom,* or *Ø*. Add the necessary prepositions.

1. a. The bus ___<u>that</u>___ we were waiting ___<u>for</u>___ was an hour late.

   b. The bus ___<u>which</u>___ we were waiting ___<u>for</u>___ was an hour late.

   c. The bus ___<u>Ø</u>___ we were waiting ___<u>for</u>___ was an hour late.

   d. The bus for ___<u>which</u>___ we were waiting ___<u>Ø</u>___ was an hour late.

2. a. The music _____ I listened _____ was pleasant.

   b. The music _____ I listened _____ was pleasant.

   c. The music _____ I listened _____ was pleasant.

   d. The music to _____ I listened _____ was pleasant.

3. a. Psychology is a subject _____ I am very interested _____.

   b. Psychology is a subject _____ I am very interested _____.

   c. Psychology is a subject _____ I am very interested _____.

   d. Psychology is a subject in _____ I am very interested _____.

4. a. The man _____ Maria was arguing _____ was very angry.

b. The man _____ Maria was arguing _____ was very angry.

c. The man _____ Maria was arguing _____ was very angry.

d. The man _____ Maria was arguing _____ was very angry.

e. The man with _____ Maria was arguing _____ was very angry.

▶ **Practice 17. Prepositions in adjective clauses.** (Chart 12-6 and Appendix 2)
Write the appropriate prepositions or **Ø**. Draw brackets around the adjective clause.

1. I enjoyed the CD [we listened ___*to*___ at Sara's apartment.]

2. I paid the shopkeeper for the glass cup [I accidentally broke ___*Ø*___.]

3. The bus we were waiting _____ was only three minutes late.

4. Mrs. Chan is someone I always enjoy talking _____ about politics.

5. I showed my roommate a text message I got from a co-worker _____.

6. One of the subjects I've been interested _____ for a long time is astronomy.

7. The people I talked _____ at the reception were interesting.

8. One of the places I want to visit _____ next year is Mexico City.

9. The website I was looking _____ had useful reviews of new computers.

10. The book I wanted _____ wasn't available at the library.

11. English grammar is one of the subjects _____ which I enjoy studying the most.

12. The friend I waved _____ didn't wave back. Maybe he just didn't see me.

▶ **Practice 18. Adjective clauses with *whose*.** (Chart 12-7)
<u>Underline</u> the adjective clause in each long sentence. Then change the long sentence into two short sentences.

1. *Long sentence:*   I know a man <u>whose daughter is a test-pilot</u>.

Short sentence 1: _____ *I know a man.* _____

Short sentence 2: _____ *His daughter is a test-pilot.* _____

2. *Long sentence:*   The woman whose husband is out of work found a job at Mel's Diner.

Short sentence 1: _____

Short sentence 2: _____

3. *Long sentence:*   The man whose wallet I found gave me a reward.

Short sentence 1: _____

Short sentence 2: _____

▶ **Practice 19. Adjective clauses with *whose*.** (Chart 12-7)
Follow these steps:

1. <u>Underline</u> the possessive word.
2. Draw an arrow to the noun it refers to.
3. Replace the possessive word with **whose**.
4. Combine the two sentences into one.

1. The firefighters are very brave. <u>Their</u> department has won many awards.

   *The firefighters **whose** deparment has won many awards are very brave.*

2. I talked to the boy. His kite was caught in a tree.

   _____

3. The family is staying in a motel. Their house burned down.

   _____

4. I watched a little girl. Her dog was chasing a ball in the park.

   _____

5. The reporter won an award. Her articles explained global warming.

   _____

6. I know a man. His daughter entered college at the age of 14.

   _____

7. We observed a language teacher. Her teaching methods included role-playing.

   _____

8. The teachers are very popular. Their methods include role-playing.

   _____

▶ **Practice 20. Meaning of adjective clauses.** (Charts 12-1 → 12-7)
Check <u>all</u> the sentences that are true.

1. The policeman who gave Henry a ticket seemed very nervous.
   a. __✓__ Henry received a ticket.
   b. _____ Henry seemed nervous.
   c. __✓__ The policeman seemed nervous.

2. A co-worker of mine whose wife is a pilot is afraid of flying.
   a. _____ My co-worker is a pilot.
   b. _____ My co-worker's wife is afraid of flying.
   c. _____ The pilot is a woman.

3. The man that delivers office supplies to our company bought a Ferrari.
   a. _____ Our company bought a Ferrari.
   b. _____ A man delivers office supplies.
   c. _____ A delivery man bought a Ferrari.

4. The doctor who took care of my father had a heart attack recently.
   a. _____ My father had a heart attack.
   b. _____ The doctor treated a heart attack patient.
   c. _____ The doctor had a heart attack.

5. The forest fire which destroyed two homes in Woodville burned for two weeks.

    a. _____ The forest fire burned for two weeks.

    b. _____ Two homes burned for two weeks.

    c. _____ The forest fire destroyed Woodville.

6. The salesman who sold my friend a used car was arrested for changing the mileage on cars.

    a. _____ My friend bought a car.

    b. _____ My friend was arrested.

    c. _____ The salesman changed the mileage on cars.

▶ **Practice 21. Adjective clauses.** (Charts 12-1 → 12-7)
Write all the possible completions: **who, that, which, whose, whom,** or **Ø.**

1. What do you say to people _____who / that_____ ask you personal questions that you don't want to answer?

2. People _____ live in New York City are called New Yorkers.

3. Tina likes the present _____ I gave her for her birthday.

4. George Washington is the president _____ picture is on a one-dollar bill.

5. Have you seen the movie _____ is playing at the Majestic Theater?

6. Do you know the woman _____ Michael is engaged to?

7. That's Tom Jenkins. He's the boy _____ parents live in Switzerland.

8. A thermometer is an instrument _____ measures temperature.

9. A high-strung person is someone _____ is always nervous.

10. The man _____ I told you about is standing over there.

11. In my country, any person _____ is 18 years old or older can vote. I turned 18 last year. The person _____ I voted for in the national election lost. I hope the next candidate for _____ I vote has better luck.

▶ **Practice 22. Reading.** (Chapter 12)
Read each paragraph. Then choose the correct completion for each sentence that follows.

Sticky Notes

    Maybe you have a sticky note in this book. Sticky notes are those small, colored papers that you can stick in books, on your own papers, on walls, and in other places. You may know them as Post-it® Notes, which was their original name. These notes are common today, but they were not a product that was planned. Like many other products, the sticky note was invented by accident.

1. This passage is about _____.
    a. paper that you can stick to something
    b. paper that you use to write letters

2. The sticky notes were a product _____.
    a. that was developed through research
    b. that was the result of an accident

    In 1970, a man whose name was Spencer Silver was working at 3M, a chemical company. The company was trying to find a strong, new glue that could hold things together. Silver created a new glue, but the glue was not strong. In fact, it was very weak. The objects he tried to stick together with the glue soon fell apart. The company didn't use the glue that Silver had created, but Silver kept it in his desk.

3. Spencer Silver invented a glue _____.
   a. that held things together
   b. that was very weak

4. The company _____.
   a. used Silver's product
   b. didn't find uses for the glue

Four years later, another 3M scientist, Arthur Fry, was singing in a choir. The bookmarks that he used to mark the songs in his songbook kept falling out. Fry wanted something that worked better and he remembered Silver's invention: the glue that was too weak.

5. Arthur Fry wanted _____.
   a. bookmarks that stuck to pages
   b. a new book of songs

6. He thought of the invention _____.
   a. that Spencer had made
   b. that 3M was using

Fry put a small amount of Silver's glue on top of his bookmarks. Success! The bookmarks on which he had placed the glue stayed on the pages. Even better, they also came off easily without damaging the pages. Fry and Silver then worked together and developed the glue which was eventually used on the Post-it ® Notes. That glue is on the back of each sticky note.

7. Fry put some glue _____.
   a. on top of the bookmarks
   b. on top of the book

8. The result was a kind of paper _____.
   a. that stuck very tightly
   b. that stuck, but could also be pulled off easily.

▶ **Practice 23. Editing.** (Chapter 12)
Correct the errors.

                    looks
1. A movie that ~~look~~ interesting opens tomorrow.

2. My family lived in a house which it was built in 1900.

3. There's the man that we saw him on TV.

4. I don't know people who their lives are carefree.

5. It is important to help people who has no money.

6. At the airport, I was waiting for friends which I hadn't seen them for a long time.

7. The woman live next door likes to relax by doing crossword puzzles every evening.

8. My teacher has two cats who their names are Ping and Pong.

9. I enjoyed the songs which we sang them.

10. The person to that you should speak is Gary Green.

Circle the five words in the puzzle. The words are the pronouns that begin adjective clauses.

The words may be horizontal, vertical, or diagonal. Note: *who* appears as a separate word in addition to appearing inside one of other words.

T	P	Y	G	E	T
W	H	O	M	S	W
T	T	T	O	O	H
Z	H	H	K	H	I
T	W	A	V	W	C
P	F	H	T	N	H

Chapter 13
Gerunds and Infinitives

▶ **Practice 1. Verb + gerund.** (Chart 13-1)
Complete the sentences with the correct form of the verbs in parentheses.

1. Joan often talks about (*move*) _____*moving*_____ overseas.

2. The Browns sometimes discuss (*live*) _____ in a smaller town.

3. Christine enjoys (*take*) _____ care of her young niece.

4. Nathan keeps (*buy*) _____ lottery tickets, but he never wins.

5. My manager considered (*give*) _____ pay raises but decided not to.

6. I always put off (*do*) _____ my math homework.

7. The students finished (*review*) _____ for the test at 3:00 A.M.

8. Ann talked about (*find*) _____ a new roommate.

9. Dana quit (*drive*) _____ after she had a serious car accident.

10. My dentist thinks about (*retire*) _____, but he enjoys his work too much.

11. Last week, Joan and David postponed (*get married*) _____ for the second time.

12. Do you mind (*work*) _____ an extra shift tonight?

▶ **Practice 2. Go + gerund.** (Chart 13-2)
Complete each sentence with a form of **go** and a word from the list.

camp	fish	sail	sightsee	skydive
✓dance	hike	shop	ski	swim

1. I love to dance. Last night, my husband and I danced for hours.

   Last night, my husband and I _____*went dancing*_____.

2. Later this afternoon, Ted is going to take a long walk in the woods.

   Ted _____ later today.

3. Yesterday, Alice visited many stores and bought some clothes and makeup.

   Yesterday, Alice _____.

4. On a hot day, I like to go to the beach and jump in the water.

   On a hot day, I like to _____.

5. My grandfather takes his fishing pole to a pond every Sunday.

   My grandfather _____ every Sunday.

6. When I visit a new city, I like to look around at the sights.

   When I visit a new city, I like to _____.

7. I love to put up a small tent by a stream, make a fire, and listen to the sounds of the forest during the night.

   I love to _____.

8. I want to take the sailboat out on the water this afternoon.

   I want to _____ this afternoon.

9. Once a year, we take our skis to our favorite mountain resort and enjoy an exciting weekend.

   Once a year, we _____ at our favorite mountain resort.

10. Last year on my birthday, my friends and I went up in an airplane, put on parachutes, and jumped out of the plane at a very high altitude.

   Last year on my birthday, my friends and I

   _____.

▶ **Practice 3. Identifying gerunds and infinitives.** (Charts 13-1 and 13-3)
Underline the gerunds and infinitives in the sentences. Circle GER for gerunds. Circle INF for infinitives.

1. Ann promised <u>to wait</u> for me.	GER	(INF)
2. I kept <u>walking</u> even though I was tired.	(GER)	INF
3. Alex offered to help me.	GER	INF
4. Karen finished cleaning up the kitchen and went to bed.	GER	INF
5. We decided to order a pizza.	GER	INF
6. David discussed quitting his job several times.	GER	INF
7. The police officers planned to work overtime during the conference.	GER	INF
8. Kevin would like to grow organic vegetables in his garden.	GER	INF

▶ **Practice 4. Verb + gerund or infinitive.** (Charts 13-1 → 13-3)
Choose the correct completion.

1. I would like (*inviting* / (*to invite*)) you and some of my other friends for dinner sometime.

2. I enjoyed (*being* / *to be*) with my family at the lake last summer.

3. My parents can't afford (*paying* / *to pay*) all of my college expenses.

4. Theresa, would you mind (*mailing* / *to mail*) this letter on your way home?

5. Do you expect (*passing* / *to pass*) this course? If so, you'd better work harder.

6. Mr. Reed refused (*considering* / *to consider*) my proposal. He had already made up his mind.

7. I wish he would consider (*accepting* / *to accept*) my proposal. I know I can do the job.

8. I don't think I'll ever finish (*reading* / *to read*) this report. It just goes on and on.

9. I would enjoy (*visiting / to visit*) you in Cairo while you're studying there.

10. I'm really sorry. I didn't mean (*hurting / to hurt*) your feelings.

11. Why do you keep (*asking / to ask*) me the same question over and over again?

12. I've decided (*looking / to look*) for another job. I'll never be happy here.

13. You need (*trying / to try*) harder if you want to get a promotion.

14. Why do you pretend (*enjoying / to enjoy*) Leon's company? I know you don't like him.

15. Let's get together tonight. I want to talk about (*opening / to open*) a new business.

16. I have a secret. Do you promise (*keeping / to keep*) it to yourself?

17. The president plans (*giving / to give*) everyone a bonus at the end of the year.

18. I have a good job, and I hope (*supporting / to support*) myself all through school.

19. I can't wait (*finishing / to finish*) work today. I'm starting my vacation tonight.

▶ **Practice 5. Verb + gerund or infinitive.** (Charts 13-1 → 13-4)
Choose the correct answer. Both answers may be correct.

1. I want _____ the comedy special on TV tonight.
   a. seeing   (b.) to see

2. I'm a people-watcher. I like _____ people in public places.
   (a.) watching   (b.) to watch

3. I've already begun _____ ideas for my new novel.
   a. collecting   b. to collect

4. A group of Chinese scientists plan _____ their discovery at the conference next spring.
   a. presenting   b. to present

5. Whenever I wash my car, it starts _____.
   a. raining   b. to rain

6. Angela and I continued _____ for several hours.
   a. talking   b. to talk

7. I love _____ on the beach during a storm.
   a. walking   b. to walk

8. I would love _____ a walk today.
   a. taking   b. to take

9. Are you sure you don't mind _____ Johnny for me while I go to the store?
   a. watching   b. to watch

10. Annie hates _____ in the rain.
    a. driving   b. to drive

11. My roommate can't stand _____ to really loud rock music.
    a. listening   b. to listen

12. I don't like _____ in front of other people.
    a. singing   b. to sing

13. Would you like _____ to the concert with us?
   a. going   b. to go

14. Charlie likes to go _____ when the weather is very windy.
   a. sailing   b. to sail

15. Most children can't wait _____ their presents on their birthday.
   a. opening   b. to open

▶ **Practice 6. Verb + gerund or infinitive.** (Charts 13-1, 13-3, and 13-4)
Complete the passages with the infinitive or gerund form of the words in parentheses.

1. Cindy wants (*go*) _____ *to go* _____ to graduate school next year. However, she can't
   afford (*pay*) _____ all the tuition, so she needs (*get*) _____ a
   scholarship. She intends (*apply*) _____ for a scholarship which is given to
   students who have done outstanding work in biology. She is optimistic, and she expects
   (*receive*) _____ it.

2. Carla and Marco are planning (*take*) _____ a vacation. Carla would love (*go*)
   _____ to a tropical beach, but Marco doesn't like hot weather. He prefers cold
   weather and would like (*go*) _____ skiing in the mountains. Although Carla
   prefers hot weather, she doesn't mind (*be*) _____ in cold weather. They will
   probably decide (*go*) _____ to the mountains this year, and Marco will enjoy
   (*ski*) _____. Next year, they'll go to the tropics and go (*swim*)
   _____ and (*sail*) _____ in the warm ocean.

3. Tom Fan was considering (*get*) _____ another job. The job that he has is a
   good one, but it doesn't have opportunities to advance. Tom decided (*tell*)
   _____ his boss, Sharon, that he was thinking about (*leave*) _____
   the company because he needed (*have*) _____ more opportunities to advance.
   Sharon offered (*create*) _____ a new position for Tom, one with more
   responsibility. Tom happily accepted the offer and agreed (*take*) _____ the new
   job as regional sales manager of a large area.

▶ **Practice 7. Gerunds and infinitives.** (Charts 13-1, 13-3, and 13-4)
Complete the sentences with the gerund or infinitive form of the verb. Some verbs may take both.

Part I. Use *work.*

1. I agreed _____ *to work* _____.
2. I put off _____ *working* _____.
3. I would love _____.
4. I thought about _____.
5. I promised _____.
6. I began _____.

7. I decided _____.
8. I offered _____.
9. I quit _____.
10. I refused _____.
11. I hoped _____.
12. I finished _____.

Part II. Use *leave*.

13. She expected _____.

14. She wanted _____.

15. She considered _____.

16. She talked about _____.

17. She postponed _____.

18. She put off _____.

19. She refused _____.

20. She needed _____.

21. She thought about _____.

22. She hoped _____.

Part III. Use *know*.

23. They seemed _____.

24. They expected _____.

25. They would like _____.

26. They don't mind _____.

27. They would love _____.

28. They want _____.

29. They can't stand _____.

30. They needed _____.

31. They appeared _____.

32. They hated _____.

▶ **Practice 8. Preposition + gerund.** (Chart 13-5)
Complete the sentences with the correct preposition. <u>Underline</u> the gerund.

Part I. Liz . . .

1. is afraid ____*of*____ <u>flying</u>.

2. apologized _____ hurting her friend's feelings.

3. believes _____ helping others.

4. is good _____ listening to her friends' concerns.

5. is tired _____ working weekends.

6. is nervous _____ walking home from work late at night.

7. dreams _____ owning a farm with horses, cows, and sheep.

8. talks _____ buying a farm in the country.

Part II. Leonard . . .

9. is responsible _____ closing the restaurant where he works at night.

10. thanked his father _____ lending him some money.

11. plans _____ becoming an accountant.

12. forgave his roommate _____ taking his car without asking.

13. insists _____ eating only fresh fruits and vegetables.

14. is looking forward _____ finishing school.

15. stopped his best friend _____ making a bad decision.

16. is worried _____ not having enough time for family and friends.

► **Practice 9. Preposition + gerund.** (Chart 13-5 and Appendix 2)
Complete the sentences. Use prepositions and gerunds.

1. Bill interrupted me. He apologized ___*for*___ that.
   Bill apologized ___*for interrupting*___ me.

2. I like to learn about other countries and cultures. I'm interested _____ that.
   I'm interested _____ about other countries and cultures.

3. I helped Ann. She thanked me _____ that.
   Ann thanked me _____ her.

4. Nadia wanted to walk to work. She insisted _____ that.
   We offered Nadia a ride, but she insisted _____ to work.

5. Nick lost my car keys. I forgave him _____ that.
   I forgave Nick _____ my car keys when he borrowed my car.

6. Sara wants to go out to eat just because she feels _____ it.
   She feels _____ out to eat.

7. I'm not a good artist. I try to draw faces, but I'm not very good _____ it.
   I'm not good _____ faces.

8. Mr. and Mrs. Reed have been saving some money for their retirement. They believe
   _____ that.
   Mr. and Mrs. Reed believe _____ money for their retirement.

9. I may forget the words I'm supposed to say in my graduation speech. I'm worried _____
   that. I'm worried _____ the words in my speech.

10. The children are going to go to Disneyland. They're excited _____ that.
    The children are excited _____ to Disneyland.

11. Their parents are going to Disneyland too. They are looking forward _____ that.
    Their parents are looking forward _____ there too.

12. Max doesn't like to stay in hotels because he is scared of heights. He is afraid _____ that.
    Max is afraid _____ in hotels.

► **Practice 10. Review.** (Charts 13-1 → 13-5)
Choose the correct completions for each group.

Part I. Completions with **ask**.

a. about asking for more money	d. to ask you about a grammar rule
b. about asking the Petersons	e. to ask for a few days off
c. asking "why"	f. to ask for directions

1. A: You look tired, Yoko. Can you stay home from work for a few days?
   B: Yes. I intend __*e*__ .

2. A: Sid, we're lost! Why don't you ask someone where the highway is?
   B: You know that I hate ____ .

3. A: You're going to talk to the boss about getting a raise, aren't you?
   B: I don't know. I'm really nervous ____

4. A: Who do you want to invite to our holiday party?
   B: I'm thinking ____.

5. A: Your little girl has a lot of questions, doesn't she?
   B: Yes, she's very curious. She keeps ____ over and over again.

6. A: Yes, do you have a question about the exercise?
   B: Yes, I do. I'd like ____.
   A: Which one?

Part II. Completions with **fix**.

g. about fixing it	j. to fix everything herself
h. at fixing things	k. to fix it myself
i. for fixing it	l. to fix it tomorrow

7. A: Are you going to fix your mother's car?
   B: No, she doesn't need help. She prefers ____.

8. A: Are you going to call the technician to fix your computer?
   B: No, I intend ____ right now.

9. A: Is the plumber coming to fix your faucet?
   B: No. My husband promised ____.

10. A: This sidewalk has been broken for a long time! When is the city going to fix it?
    B: They've been talking ____ for months, but they never do.

11. A: Oh, I'm so sorry! I didn't mean to break your chair.
    B: Don't worry about it. Jerry will fix it. He's excellent ____.

12. A: My car has a real problem. It's very hard to steer.
    B: Did you know that the company is responsible ____? All the cars have been recalled, and the company has to fix them for free.

▶ **Practice 11. Review.** (Charts 13-1 → 13-5)
Choose the correct completion in each pair. More than one answer may be possible.

(1) I am a procrastinator. A procrastinator is a person who puts off (*doing* / to do) something that she hates (*doing* / to do) until a later time. Unfortunately, although the person may intend (*doing* / to do) the task soon, it may not be done for a long time.

(2) Here's an example. I received a beautiful silk sweater from my Aunt Sarah. I meant (*write* / *to write*) to her immediately to thank her, but I postponed (*doing* / to do) so. I kept (*thinking* / to think), "I'll write tomorrow." After a month, I hadn't written to her, and I was too embarrassed to call her. Finally I wrote this:

Dear Aunt Sarah,

(3) I apologize (*for being* / to be) so late with this note. I want (*to thank* / thanking) you for (*sending* / to send) me the lovely blue silk sweater. I will certainly enjoy (*wearing* / to wear) it to parties and special events. In fact, I'm planning (*wearing* / to wear) it to your birthday dinner next week.

(4) I really look forward (*to seeing* / to see) you then. Please forgive me (*for taking* / to take) so long to say thank you.

Complete the sentences with the appropriate gerund or infinitive of the word in *italics*. Some sentences also require a preposition.

1. Matthew wants to *go* to a different doctor for his back pain. He's considering __*going*__ to a specialist.

2. Jim would rather walk than *drive* to work. Instead _____*of driving*_____, Jim walks along bike trails to his office.

3. I never *watch* commercials on TV. In fact, I can't stand _____ TV commercials, so I generally watch only shows that I've recorded.

4. Joanne's hobby is *cooking*. She loves _____ gourmet meals for friends and relatives.

5. Martina is nervous about *going* to the dentist for a filling. She has been afraid _____ to the dentist since she was a little girl.

6. Walter's dream is to *become* a doctor in a rural area. He has dreamed _____ a doctor since he was hospitalized as a child.

7. Nathan *has* a chocolate milkshake every afternoon for a snack. He often feels like _____ two, but he doesn't.

8. Every morning, rain or shine, Debbie rises early and stretches. Then she goes outside and *runs* for 30 minutes. Every morning, Debbie goes _____ for half an hour.

9. Mark *washes* all his clothes in hot water. Although his roommates tell him hot water could damage some clothes, he doesn't listen. He insists _____ all his clothes in hot water.

10. The little girl didn't see the car rolling slowly toward her. No one was in it, but fortunately a neighbor jumped into the car and stopped it before it could *hit* her. The neighbor stopped the car _____ the girl.

11. When Rita came to work, her eyes *were* red and she appeared upset, but she said everything was okay. Later, she was laughing and looked more relaxed. Rita seemed _____ better.

12. Tang has been studying medicine abroad for two years and hasn't *seen* his family in all that time. He is going home next week and is very excited _____ his family.

► **Practice 13. *By* + gerund.** (Chart 13-6)
Describe what the people did by using *by* + a gerund.

1. MARY: How did you comfort the child?
   SUE: I held him in my arms.
   Sue comforted the child _____*by holding*_____ him in her arms.

2. PAT: How did you improve your vocabulary?
   NADIA: I read a lot of books.
   Nadia improved her vocabulary _____ a lot of books.

3. KIRK: How did Grandma entertain the children?
   SALLY: She told them a story.
   Grandma entertained the children _____ them a story.

4. MASAKO: How did you improve your English?
   PEDRO: I watched TV a lot.
   Pedro improved his English _____ TV a lot.

5. JEFFREY: How did you catch up with the bus?
   JIM: I ran as fast as I could.
   Jim caught up with the bus _____ as fast as he could.

6. MR. LEE: How did you earn your children's respect?
   MR. COY: I treated them with respect at all times.
   Mr. Coy earned his children's respect _____ them with respect at all times.

▶ **Practice 14. By + gerund.** (Chart 13-6)
Complete the sentences with **by** + an appropriate verb from the list.

count	follow	look	pour	save	stretch	✓take	work

1. I arrived on time _____ *by taking* _____ a taxi instead of a bus.

2. I put out the fire _____ water on it.

3. Giraffes can reach the leaves at the tops of trees _____ their long necks.

4. I finished writing my final paper _____ all through the night.

5. Sylvia was able to buy an expensive condominium _____ her money for four years.

6. I cooked the noodles correctly _____ the directions on the package.

7. You can find out the temperature in any city in the world _____ it up on the Internet.

8. You can figure out how old a tree is _____ its rings.

► **Practice 15. *By* vs. *with.*** (Chart 13-6)
Circle all the correct completions.

1. Ole went to Quebec by _____.
   a. bus
   b. a bus
   c. his feet
   d. plane
   e. taxi
   f. train

2. Kim ate dinner with _____.
   a. a fork
   b. a spoon
   c. chopsticks
   d. fork
   e. hand
   f. knife

3. Ali sent the information by _____.
   a. a phone
   b. email
   c. fax
   d. mistake
   e. his hand
   f. phone

4. Sid cleaned the kitchen with _____.
   a. a broom
   b. a mop
   c. hand
   d. soap and water
   e. disinfectant
   f. a cloth

► **Practice 16. Gerund as subject; *It* + infinitive.** (Chart 13-7)
Complete the sentences by using a gerund as the subject or *it* + infinitive. Add *is* where appropriate. Use the verbs in the list.

complete	eat	live
drive	✓learn	swim

1. a. _____It is_____ easy for anyone _____to learn_____ how to cook an egg.

   b. _____Learning_____ how to cook an egg _____is_____ easy for anyone.

2. a. _____ nutritious food _____ important for your health.

   b. _____ important for your health _____ nutritious food.

3. a. _____ on the wrong side of the road _____ against the law.

   b. _____ against the law _____ on the wrong side of the road.

4. a. _____ fun for both children and adults _____ in the warm sea.

   b. _____ in the warm sea _____ fun for both children and adults.

5. a. _____ expensive _____ in a dormitory?

   b. _____ in a dormitory expensive?

6. a. _____ difficult _____ these sentences correctly?

   b. _____ these sentences correctly difficult?

► **Practice 17. Purpose: *to* vs. *for.*** (Chart 13-8)
Rewrite the sentences. Use *it . . . for someone + an infinitive phrase.* Use the adjective in parentheses.

1. Shy people have a hard time meeting others at social events. (*difficult*)

   _____*It is difficult for shy people to meet*_____ others at social events.

2. In many cultures, young children sleep in the same room as their parents. (*customary*)

   In many cultures, _____
   in the same room as their parents.

3. Airline pilots need to have good eyesight. (*necessary*)

   _____ good eyesight.

4. Many teenagers can't wake up early. (*hard*)

   _____ early.

5. Elderly people need to keep their minds active. (*important*)

   _____ their minds active.

6. People don't like listening to monotone speakers. (*boring*)

   _____ to monotone speakers.

7. Scientists will never know the origin of every disease in the world. (*impossible*)

   _____ the origin of every disease in
   the world.

► **Practice 18. Purpose: *to* vs. *for.*** (Chart 13-9)
Complete the sentences with *to* or *for*.

1. Yesterday, I called the doctor's office . . .

   a. ___*for*___ an appointment.

   b. ___*to*___ make an appointment.

   c. _____ get a prescription.

   d. _____ a prescription.

   e. _____ ask a question.

   f. _____ get some advice.

   g. _____ some advice.

2. Yesterday, Chuck stayed after class . . .

   a. _____ talk with the teacher.

   b. _____ a talk with the teacher.

   c. _____ some extra help.

   d. _____ finish a project.

   e. _____ work with other students.

   f. _____ a meeting with other students.

   g. _____ help plan a class party.

► **Practice 19. Purpose: *to* vs. *for.*** (Chart 13-9)
Complete the sentences with *to* or *for*.

1. We wear coats in cold weather ___*to*___ keep warm.

2. We wear coats in cold weather ___*for*___ warmth.

3. Mark contacted a lawyer _____ legal advice.

4. Mark contacted a lawyer _____ discuss a legal problem.

5. Sam went to the hospital _____ an operation.

6. We hired a teenager _____ cut my grandmother's grass twice a month.

7. Frank went to the library _____ review for the test.

8. I play tennis twice a week _____ fun and exercise.

9. Jennifer used some medicine _____ cure an infection on her arm.

10. I lent Yvette some money _____ her school expenses.

11. I asked my manager _____ permission to take the rest of the day off.

▶ **Practice 20. *(In order) to.*** (Chart 13-9)
Combine the given phrases in *italics* to create sentences using (*in order*) *to*.

1. *watch the news + turn on the TV*

   After he got home from work, Jack _____ turned on the TV (in order) to watch the news. _____

2. *wash his clothes + go to the laundromat*

   Every weekend Martin _____

   _____

3. *run + get to class on time*

   Every morning Jeannette _____

   _____

4. *let in some fresh air + open the bedroom windows*

   Every night I _____

5. *ask them for some money + call his parents*

   Sometimes Pierre _____

6. *listen to a baseball game + have the radio on*

   Some afternoons at work, my co-workers _____

   _____

7. *study in peace and quiet + go to the library*

   Some evenings, I _____

▶ **Practice 21. *Too* vs. *enough.*** (Chart 13-10)
Complete the sentences with the words in parentheses and *too* or *enough*.

1. I have a tight schedule tomorrow, so I can't go to the park.

   a. (*time*) I don't have _____ enough time to go _____ to the park.

   b. (*busy*) I'm _____ too busy to go _____ to the park.

2. I'm pretty short. I can't touch the ceiling.

   a. (*tall*) I'm not _____ to touch the ceiling.

   b. (*short*) I'm _____ to touch the ceiling.

3. Marcus has been out of work for months. He can't pay any of his bills.

   a. (*money*) Marcus doesn't have _____ to pay his bills.

   b. (*poor*) Marcus is _____ to pay his bills.

4. This tea is very hot. I need to wait a while until I can drink it.

   a. (*hot*) This tea is _____ to drink.

   b. (*cool*) This tea isn't _____ to drink.

5. I feel sick. I don't want to eat anything.

 a. (*sick*) I feel _____ to eat anything.

 b. (*well*) I don't feel _____ to eat anything.

6. Nora is only six years old. She can't stay home by herself.

 a. (*old*) Nora _____ to stay home by herself.

 b. (*young*) Nora _____ to stay home by herself.

▶ **Practice 22. *Too* vs. *enough*.** (Chart 13-10)
Complete the sentences with *too*, *enough*, or Ø.

1. I think this problem is ____*Ø*____ important ____*enough*____ to require our immediate attention.

2. Nina is not ____*too*____ tired ____*Ø*____ to finish the project before she goes home.

3. You can do this math problem by yourself. You're _____ smart _____ to figure it out.

4. Our company is _____ small _____ to start new branches overseas.

5. My niece doesn't drive yet. She's _____ young _____ to get a driver's license.

6. Robert is an amazing runner. His coach thinks he is _____ good _____ to begin training for an Olympic marathon.

7. Look at the children watching the clowns. They can't sit still. They're _____ excited _____ to stay in their chairs.

8. The heat outside is terrible! It's _____ hot _____ to fry an egg on the sidewalk!

▶ **Practice 23. Gerund vs. infinitive.** (Chapter 13)
Complete the passage with the correct form of the verbs in parentheses.

Generalizations About Extroverts and Introverts

 An extrovert is someone who appears active and confident and who enjoys (*be*)

_____ with other people. This is the opposite of an introvert, who is quiet and
  1

shy and does not want (*spend*) _____ a lot of time with other people .
  2

 An extrovert gets energy by (*be*) _____ around other people. An introvert
  3

gets energy from (*be*) _____ alone.
  4

 Extroverts try (*find*) _____ social situations because they like interacting
  5

with people. Introverts often avoid (*be*) _____ in social situations because they
  6

are not comfortable in them.

An extrovert prefers (*talk*) _____ with someone else instead of (*sit*)

_____ alone and (*think*) _____. In fact, extroverts
    8   9

sometimes seem (*think*) _____ and speak at the same time, unlike introverts
                            10

who think about their words before (*speak*) _____.
                                               11

Extroverts, are often good at (*make*) _____ social conversation, while
                                          12

introverts — who may be shy at first — would like (*discuss*) _____ ideas instead.
                                                                    13

▶ **Practice 24. Gerund vs. infinitive.** (Chapter 13)
Complete the sentences with the gerund or infinitive form of the word in parentheses.

1. (*study*) _____*Studying*_____ English can be fun.

2. My boss makes a habit of (*write*) _____ nice emails to her employees when

   they've done a good job.

3. From the earth, the sun and the moon appear (*be*) _____ almost the same size.

4. A: I don't like airplanes.

   B: Why? Are you afraid of (*fly*) _____?

   A: No, I'm afraid of (*crash*) _____.

5. A: Let's quit (*argue*) _____. Let's just agree (*disagree*)

   _____. We can still be friends.

   B: Sounds good to me. And I apologize for (*raise*) _____ my voice. I

   didn't mean (*yell*) _____ at you.

   A: That's okay. I didn't intend (*get*) _____ angry at you either.

6. A: Do you think that it's important for children (*have*) _____ chores

   around the house?

   B: Yes, I do. I think it's essential for them (*learn*) _____ about

   responsibility that way.

7. A: What do you feel like (*do*) _____ this afternoon?

   B: I feel like (*go*) _____ (*shop*) _____ at the mall.

   What about you?

   A: I don't mind (*shop*) _____ at the mall when it's quiet, but there's a sale

   today and it will be too crowded.

8. A: Have you called Alexa yet?

   B: No, I keep (*put*) _____ it off?

   A: Why?

   B: She's mad at me for (*forget*) _____ (*send*) _____

   her a card on her birthday.

Correct the errors.

                 to buy

1. I decided not ~~buying~~ a new car.

2. The Johnsons are considering to sell their antique store.

3. Sam finally finished build his vacation home in the mountains.

4. My wife and I go to dancing at the community center every Saturday night.

5. Suddenly, it began to raining and the wind started to blew.

6. The baby is afraid be away from her mother for any length of time.

7. I am excited for start college this September.

8. You can send your application with fax.

9. My country is too beautiful.

10. Is exciting to drive a sports car.

11. My grandparents enjoy to traveling across the country in a motor home.

12. Elena made this sweater with her hands.

13. Running it is one of the sports we can participate in at school.

14. Swim with a group of people is more enjoyable than swim alone.

15. Meeting new people it is interesting.

Complete the puzzle. Use the clues to find the correct words. All are grammar points from Chapter 13.

Across

2. The best way to eat pizza is _____ your fingers.

4. Sorry! I am _____ tired to go out tonight.

5. Would you mind _____ me up for work tomorrow? My car is being fixed.

6. Ben buys things at the mall on weekends when he goes _____.

9. We went to the lecture early in order to _____ good seats.

10. My family and I enjoy _____ together in our small sailboat.

11. The only way to get to the small island is _____ boat.

12. It's not difficult for Carlos to _____ the guitar because he is a professional guitarist.

13. Bob is 21. He is old _____ to vote.

Down

1. We are considering _____ our vacation plans. We may go in July instead of in June.

3. The Stein family is thinking about _____ to a larger house.

7. Margo expects to _____ from college next June.

8. I finished _____ at midnight and went right to bed.

Chapter 14

Noun Clauses

▶ **Practice 1. Questions vs. noun clauses.** (Chart 14-1)
If the sentence contains a noun clause, <u>underline</u> it and circle *noun clause*. If the question word introduces a question, circle *question*. Add appropriate final punctuation: a period (**.**) or a question mark (**?**).

1.	I don't know <u>where Yuri lives</u>**.**	(noun clause)	question
2.	Where does Yuri live**?**	noun clause	(question)
3.	I don't understand why Sofia left	noun clause	question
4.	Why did Sofia leave	noun clause	question
5.	When did Oliver leave	noun clause	question
6.	I don't know when Oliver left	noun clause	question
7.	What does "calm" mean	noun clause	question
8.	Tarik knows what "calm" means	noun clause	question
9.	I don't know how long the earth has existed	noun clause	question
10.	How long has the earth existed	noun clause	question
11.	Where is Patagonia	noun clause	question
12.	I don't know where Patagonia is	noun clause	question

▶ **Practice 2. Noun clauses that begin with a question word.** (Chart 14-2)
Answer the questions using noun clauses.

1. A: Where does Helen work?

   B: I don't know where _____*Helen works*_____.

2. A: What did Adam say?

   B: I didn't hear what _____.

3. Why are we doing this?

   I don't know why _____.

4. When does the new semester start?

   Tell me when _____.

5. Where did everyone go?

   I don't know where _____.

6. What do people believe?

   We don't know what _____.

7. Who believes that story?

I don't know who _____.

8. Whose cell phone is ringing?

I don't know whose _____.

▶ **Practice 3. Noun clauses that begin with a question word.** (Chart 14-2)
Complete the noun clauses.

1. Vince doesn't live near me. Do you know where _____*Vince lives*_____?

2. I don't know that woman. Do you know who _____*that woman is*_____?

3. Henri did something. Do you know what _____?

4. I don't know her phone number. Do you know what _____?

5. These are someone's keys. Do you know whose _____?

6. Clara met someone. Do you know who _____?

7. Carlo is absent today. Do you know why _____?

8. What time is it? Do you know what time _____?

9. Sam is studying something. Do you know what _____?

10. Someone called. Do you know who _____?

11. Ms. Gray will call later today. Do you know when _____?

12. The president is going to say something. Do you know what _____
_____?

13. Who is in that room? Do you know who _____?

14. What is in that drawer? Do you what _____?

15. A GPS system doesn't cost a lot of money, does it? Do you know how much _____
_____?

▶ **Practice 4. Information questions and noun clauses.** (Chart 14-2)
Complete the question and noun clause forms of the given sentences.

1. Marcos left at 11:00.

When _____*did Marcos leave?*_____

Could you tell me _____*when Marcos left?*_____

2. He said good-bye.

What _____

I didn't hear _____

3. The post office is on Second Street.

Where _____

Could you please tell me _____

4. It's half-past six.

What time _____

Could you please tell me _____

5. David arrived two days ago.

When _____

I don't know _____

6. Ana is from Peru.

What country _____

I'd like to know _____

7. Kathy was absent because she was ill.

Why _____ absent?

Do you know _____ absent?

8. Pedro lives next door.

Who _____ next door?

Do you know _____ next door?

9. Someone's car is in the driveway.

Whose _____ in the driveway?

Do you know _____ in the driveway?

10. These books are someone's.

Whose _____

Do you know _____

▶ **Practice 5. Noun clauses.** (Chart 14-2)
Complete each sentence with a noun clause made from the list. There is one extra word in each list.

1. *who, to, did, Helen, talked*

Who did Helen talk to? Do you know _____*who Helen talked to*_____?

2. *does, who, lives*

Who lives in that apartment? Do you know _____ in that apartment?

3. *he, what, said, did*

What did he say? Tell me _____.

4. *has, Pat, does, what kind of car*

What kind of car does Pat have? I can't remember _____.

5. *how, their children, are, old, do*

How old are their children? I can't ever remember _____.

6. *why, did, you, said*

Why did you say that? I don't understand _____ that.

7. *I, do, can, catch, where*

Where can I catch the bus? Could you please tell me _____
the bus?

8. *does, what, this word, means*

What does this word mean? Could you please tell me _____?

► **Practice 6. Noun clauses.** (Chart 14-2)
Choose the correct completion.

1. Why _____ so late?
   a. you are
   b. are you

2. I'd like to know why _____ so late.
   a. you are
   b. are you

3. Tell us where _____ on your vacation, Pam.
   a. you went
   b. did you go

4. I went sailing in the Bahamas. Where _____ on your vacation?
   a. you went
   b. did you go

5. I couldn't understand the professor. What _____?
   a. she said
   b. did she say

6. I couldn't understand her either. I have no idea what _____.
   a. she said
   b. did she say

7. What _____?
   a. this word means
   b. does this word mean

8. I don't know what _____.
   a. it means
   b. does it mean

9. Do you know what _____?
   a. a bumblebee is
   b. is a bumblebee

10. Ask Helen. She knows a lot of words. Hey, Helen. What _____?
    a. a bumblebee is
    b. is a bumblebee

11. Who _____ on the phone?
    a. was that
    b. that was

12. I don't know who _____. The person hung up.
    a. was that
    b. that was

► **Practice 7. Noun clauses.** (Chart 14-2)
Read the email message. Choose the correct completion in each pair.

Hi Mom and Dad:

(1) Well, after one week in Mexico, I'm very glad to be here, but I also feel a little lost at times. I thought that I knew some Spanish, but really, I can't understand what (*people are saying* / *are people saying*). Even though I have a map, I can't read it very well, so I don't know where (*are all the buildings* / *all the buildings are*). I know when (*my classes start* / *do my classes start*) — next Monday — and where (*I register* / *do I register*). I know what classes (*am I taking* / *I am taking*), but, of course, I don't know who (*my professors will be* / *will be my professors*).

(2) Last night I felt lonely. ☹ I don't know how long (*it will take* / *will it take*) to make new friends, and I was wondering why (*did I come* / *I came*) here. But today I feel much better and I know why (*am I* / *I am*) here: I'm going to study another language and learn about another culture, and I'm going to be making new friends.

Love, Pat ☺

Change each *yes/no* question to a noun clause.

1. YES/NO QUESTION: Is Tom coming?

   NOUN CLAUSE: I wonder _____*if / whether Tom is coming*_____ .

2. YES/NO QUESTION: Has Jin finished medical school yet?

   NOUN CLAUSE: I don't know _____ .

3. YES/NO QUESTION: Does Daniel have any time off soon?

   NOUN CLAUSE: I don't know _____ .

4. YES/NO QUESTION: Is the flight on time?

   NOUN CLAUSE: Can you tell me _____ ?

5. YES/NO QUESTION: Is there enough gas in the car?

   NOUN CLAUSE: Do you know _____ ?

6. YES/NO QUESTION: Is Yuki married?

   NOUN CLAUSE: I can't remember _____ .

7. YES/NO QUESTION: Are the Nelsons going to move?

   NOUN CLAUSE: I wonder _____ .

8. YES/NO QUESTION: Did Khaled change jobs?

   NOUN CLAUSE: I don't know _____ .

▶ **Practice 9. Noun clauses.** (Chart 14-3)
Complete the sentences using noun clauses.

1. A: Are you going to need help moving furniture to your new apartment?

   B: I don't know _____*if I'm going to need*_____ help. Thanks for asking. I'll let you know.

2. A: What do you want for dinner tonight?

   B: I'm sorry. I couldn't hear you with the TV on.

   A: I want to know _____ for dinner tonight.

3. A: Is there going to be a movie on this flight?

   B: I'll ask the flight attendant. Excuse me, we're wondering _____

   _____ a movie on this flight.

4. A: Where do birds go in hurricanes?

   B: I have no idea _____ in hurricanes.

5. A: Can I borrow the car, Dad?

   B: I'll tell you later _____ the car.

6. A: Has Nasser already left the party?

   B: Sorry, it's so noisy here. I didn't catch that.

   A: I need to know _____ the party.

7. A: Why did Harold leave town so fast?

   B: I really don't know _____ town so fast.

▶ **Practice 10. Noun clauses.** (Chart 14-3)
Complete the sentences with the correct form of the verbs. Pay special attention to the use of final *-s/-es*.

1. Does it rain a lot here?

   Could you tell me if it _____rains_____ a lot here?

2. How hot does it get in the summer?

   Could you tell me how hot it _____ in the summer?

3. What do people like to do here?

   Could you tell me what people _____ to do here?

4. Does bus number 10 run on holidays?

   Could you tell me if bus number 10 _____ on holidays?

5. Do the buses run on holidays?

   Could you tell me if the buses _____ on holidays?

6. How long does it take to get to the city?

   Could you tell me how long it _____ to get to the city?

7. What do people enjoy most about this area?

   Could you tell me what people _____ most about this area?

8. Does it seem like an expensive place to live?

   Could you tell me if it _____ like an expensive place to live?

▶ **Practice 11. *That*-clauses.** (Chart 14-4)
Choose the correct completion from Column B.

Column A

1. Johnny's hungry. I guess that _____.

2. Why are you afraid to fly on planes? Read this report. It proves that _____.

3. Our son has nightmares. He often dreams that _____.

4. The police assume that _____.

5. I have to get up very early tomorrow, so I suppose _____.

6. I always know when Paul is nervous. Have you ever noticed that _____?

7. I used to think that older people couldn't learn a new language, but now I realize that _____.

8. I'm not sure about the benefits of coffee, but I know that _____.

Column B

a. monsters are chasing him

b. he always twists his moustache when he is anxious

c. he didn't eat much lunch

d. they can

e. green tea has some healthy ingredients

f. flying is a lot safer than driving

g. an experienced thief stole the money

h. I should go to bed early tonight

▶ **Practice 12. *That*-clauses.** (Charts 14-4 and 14-5)
Add ***that*** to the sentences at the appropriate places to mark the beginning of a noun clause.

1. I'm sorry ⌃ you won't be here for Joe's party.
     that

2. I predict Jim and Sue will get married before the end of the year.

3. I'm surprised you sold your car.

4. Are you certain Mr. McVay won't be here tomorrow?

5. Did you notice Marco shaved off his mustache?

6. It's a fact hot air rises.

7. A: How do you know it's going to be nice tomorrow?
   B: I heard the weather report.
   A: So? The weather report is often wrong, you know. I'm still worried it'll rain on our picnic.

8. A: I heard Professor Samson is leaving the university.
   B: Really? Why?
   A: Some people assume he is going to retire. But I doubt it. I think he is going to do research and writing.
   B: This is not good news! He's a great teacher.

▶ **Practice 13. *That*-clauses.** (Chart 14-5)
Write two sentences for each passage. Make noun clauses, and include the words in parentheses.

1. The Jensens celebrated the graduation of their granddaughter Alice from the university. After graduation, she was offered a good job in chemical research in a nearby town.

   The Jensens (*be pleased*) _are pleased that their granddaughter graduated from the university_ .

   They (*be glad*) __are glad that she was offered a good job__ .

2. One night on the news, Po's parents heard about a big fire at Po's university. All the students had to leave their dorms. Po's parents thought that maybe Po had been injured. When Po called them about an hour later, they felt relieved.

   At first, Po's parents (*be worried*)

   _____ .

   Then, they (*be happy*) _____ .

3. Kyle didn't study for his math exam. Afterward, he thought he had failed, but actually, he got one of the highest grades in the class. His teacher had known he would do well and praised him for earning such a high grade.

   Kyle (*be afraid*) _____ .

   Kyle's teacher (*not, be surprised*) _____ .

4. Karen lent her cousin Mark some money. He said that he needed it to pay the rent. Then she heard that he had left town. She feels upset that Mark lied to her. She regrets lending him money.

   Karen (*be angry*) _____ .

   Karen (*be sorry*) _____ .

5. People used to think that strenuous exercise was bad for the heart. However, now scientists have proven the opposite: strenuous exercise can be good for the heart. In addition, people used to think that eating a lot of red meat was good for the heart. Now doctors know that eating a lot of red meat is bad for the heart.

It is a fact (*exercise*) _____.

It is true (*eating a lot of red meat*) _____

_____ .

▶ **Practice 14. Substituting *so* for a *that*-clause.** (Chart 14-6)
Give the meaning of *so* by writing a *that*-clause.

1. A: Does Alice have a car?

   B: I don't think *so*. (= I don't think ____*that Alice has a car*____.)

2. A: Is the library open on Sunday?

   B: I believe *so*. (= I believe _____.)

3. A: Does Ann speak Spanish?

   B: I don't think *so*. (= I don't think _____.)

4. A: Did Alex pass his French course?

   B: I think *so*. (= I think _____.)

5. A: Is Mr. Kozari going to be at the meeting?

   B: I hope *so*. (= I hope _____.)

6. A: Are these pants clean?

   B: I believe *so*. (= I believe _____.)

▶ **Practice 15. Quoted speech.** (Chart 14-7)
All of the sentences contain quoted speech. Punctuate them by adding quotation marks ("...."), commas (,), periods (.), and question marks (?). Use capital letters as necessary.

Example: My roommate said the door is open could you close it
     My roommate said, "The door is open. Could you close it?"

1. Alex asked do you smell smoke

2. Something is burning he said

3. He asked do you smell smoke something is burning

4. Do you smell smoke he asked something is burning

5. Rachel said the game starts at seven

6. The game starts at seven we should leave here at six she said

7. She said the game starts at seven we should leave here at six can you be ready to leave then

▶ **Practice 16. Quoted speech.** (Charts 14-7 and 14-8)
Punctuate the quoted passage. Add quotation marks ("..."), commas (,), periods (.), and question marks (?). Use capital letters as necessary.

One day my friend Laura and I were sitting in her apartment. We were having a cup of tea together and talking about the terrible earthquake that had just occurred in Iran. Laura asked me, "Have you ever been in an earthquake?"

Yes, I have I replied.

Was it a big earthquake she asked.

I've been in several earthquakes, and they've all been small ones I answered. Have you ever been in an earthquake?

There was an earthquake in my village five years ago Laura said. I was in my house. Suddenly the ground started shaking. I grabbed my little brother and ran outside. Everything was moving. I was scared to death. And then suddenly it was over.

I'm glad you and your brother weren't hurt I said.

Yes, we were very lucky. Has everyone in the world felt an earthquake sometime in their lives Laura wondered. Do earthquakes occur everywhere on the earth?

Those are interesting questions I said but I don't know the answers.

► **Practice 17. Reported speech: changing pronouns and possessive words.**
(Chart 14-8)
Complete the sentences with the correct pronouns or possessive words.

1. Mr. Lee said, "I'm not happy with my new assistant."

   Mr. Lee said that ____*he*____ wasn't happy with ____*his*____ new assistant.

2. Tom said to his wife, "My parents invited us over for dinner next weekend."

   Tom said that _____ parents had invited _____ over for dinner

   next weekend.

3. The little girl said, "I don't want to wear my good shoes to the party."

   The little girl said that _____ didn't want to wear _____ good

   shoes to the party.

4. Jim said, "A police officer gave Anna and me tickets for jaywalking and told us to cross the

   street with the traffic lights at the pedestrian crosswalk."

   Jim said that a police officer had given Anna and _____ tickets for jaywalking

   and told _____ to cross the street with the traffic lights at the crosswalk.

5. The Johnsons said to me, "We will send you an email when we arrive in Nepal."

   The Johnsons said that _____ would send _____ an email when

   _____ arrived in Nepal.

6. Jane said, "I want my daughter to feel good about herself."

   Jane said that _____ wanted _____ daughter to feel good about

   herself.

7. Mary and Jack said to me, "We are going to be out of town on the day of your party."

   Mary and Jack said that _____ were going to be out of town on the day of

   _____ party.

8. Bob said to us, "We will join you after we take my mother to the airport."

   Bob told us that _____ would join _____ after

   _____ took _____ mother to the airport.

► **Practice 18. Verb forms in reported speech.** (Chart 14-9)
Complete each sentence with the correct form of the verb.

1. Juan said, "I will meet you at the corner of Fifth and Broadway."

   Formal: Juan said (that) he ____*would meet*____ ⎤
   Informal: Juan said (that) he ____*will meet*____ ⎦ us at the corner of Fifth and Broadway.

2. Maria said, "I'm going to be about 15 minutes late for work."

   Formal: Maria said she _____ ⎤
   Informal: Maria said she _____ ⎦ about 15 minutes late for work.

3. Roberto said, "My new car has a dent."

   Formal: Roberto said his new car _____ ⎤
   Informal: Roberto said his new car _____ ⎦ a dent.

4. Phil said, "I need to borrow some money."

   Formal: Phil said he _____

   Informal: Phil said he _____ to borrow some money.

5. Sandy said, "I have flown on an airplane only once."

   Formal: Sandy said she _____

   Informal: Sandy said she _____ on an airplane only once.

6. Sami and Jun said, "We are planning a surprise party for Naoko."

   Formal: Sami and Jun said they _____

   Informal: Sami and Jun said they _____ a surprise party for Naoko.

7. Naoko said, "I don't want any gifts for my birthday."

   Formal: Naoko said she _____

   Informal: Naoko said she _____ any gifts for her birthday.

8. Ms. Wall said, "I can take care of your kids next weekend."

   Formal: Ms. Wall said she _____

   Informal: Ms. Wall said she _____ of my kids next weekend.

▶ **Practice 19. Verb forms in reported speech.** (Chart 14-9)

Complete the sentences. Write the opposite of the quoted speech. Use formal sequence of tenses.

1. A: I have a lot of time.
   B: Oh? I misunderstood you. I heard you say ____*(that) you didn't have*____ a lot of time.

2. A: I found my credit cards.
   B: I misunderstood you. I heard you say _____ your credit cards.

3. A: The Smiths didn't cancel their party.
   B: I misunderstood you. I heard you say _____ their party.

4. A: It will rain tomorrow.
   B: I misunderstood you. I heard you say _____ tomorrow.

5. A: The Whites didn't get a new car.
   B: I misunderstood you. I heard you say _____ a new car.

6. A: Mei exercises every day.
   B: I misunderstood you. I heard you say _____ every day.

7. A: My computer is working.
   B: I misunderstood you. I heard you say _____
   _____ .

8. A: Ali isn't coming on Friday.
   B: I misunderstood you. I heard you say _____ on Friday.

► **Practice 20. Reporting questions.** (Chart 14-10)
Change the quoted questions to reported questions. Use formal sequence of tenses.

1. Eric said to me, "How old are you?"

   Eric asked me _____*how old I was*_____ .

2. Ms. Rush said to Mr. Long, "Are you going to be at the meeting?"

   Ms. Rush asked Mr. Long _____*if he was going to be*_____ at the meeting.

3. Larry said to Ms. Soo, "Do you have time to help me?"

   Larry asked Ms. Soo _____ time to help him.

4. Don said to Robert, "Did you change your mind about going to college?"

   Don asked Robert _____ mind about going to college.

5. Igor said to me, "How long have you been a teacher?"

   Igor asked me _____ a teacher.

6. I said to Tina, "Can you speak Swahili?"

   I asked Tina _____ Swahili.

7. Kathy said to Mr. May, "Will you be in your office around three?"

   Kathy asked Mr. May _____ around three.

8. The teacher said to Ms. Chang, "Why are you laughing?"

   The teacher asked Ms. Chang _____ .

9. My uncle said to me, "Have you ever considered a career in business?"

   My uncle asked me _____ a career in business.

► **Practice 21. Quoting questions.** (Chart 14-10)
Change the reported speech to quotations.

1. Eric asked me if I had ever gone skydiving.

   Eric asked, ____"*Have you ever gone skydiving*?"_____

2. Chris wanted to know if I would be at the meeting.

   Chris asked, _____

3. Kate wondered whether I was going to quit my job.

   Kate asked, _____

4. Anna asked her friend where his car was.

   Anna asked, _____

5. Brian asked me what I had done after class yesterday.

   Brian asked, _____

6. Luigi asked me if I knew Italian.

   Luigi asked, _____

7. Debra wanted to know if I could pick up her daughter at school.

   Debra asked, _____

8. My boss wanted to know why I wasn't working at my desk.

   My boss asked me, _____

► **Practice 22. Reporting questions.** (Charts 14-9 → 14-10)
Look at the picture and complete the sentences with noun clauses. Use verbs that are appropriate for later reporting (rather than immediate reporting).

1. Why did you come here?
2. Have you met many people?
3. What are you going to study?
4. How long will you stay?
5. How do you like it here?
6. Where are you from?
7. Are the local people friendly to you?
8. How did you choose this school?
9. Do you like the weather here?

A new student, Mr. Sheko, joined an English class. The teacher asked the students to interview him. Later, Mr. Sheko told his friend about the interview.

1. They asked me _____ *why I had to come here.* _____

2. They asked me _____

3. They asked me _____

4. They asked me _____

5. They asked me _____

6. They asked me _____

7. They asked me _____

8. They asked me _____

9. They asked me _____

► **Practice 23. Reported speech.** (Charts 14-9 → 14-10)
Complete the reported speech sentences. Use formal sequence of tenses.

1. David said to me, "I'm going to call you on Friday."

   David said _____ *(that) he was going to call me* _____
   on Friday.

2. John said to Ann, "I have to talk to you."

   John told Ann _____

   _____ .

I have to talk to you.

3. Diane said to me, "I can meet you after work."

   Diane said _____ after work.

4. Maria said to Bob, "I wrote you a note."

   Maria told Bob _____

   a note.

I wrote you a note.

5. Anita asked Mike, "When will I see you again?"

   Anita asked Mike when _____

   _____ again.

6. Laura said to George, "What are you doing?"

   Laura asked George _____

   _____ .

▶ **Practice 24. Say vs. tell vs. ask.** (Chart 14-10)
Complete the sentences with **said**, **told**, or **asked**.

1. Ava _____*told*_____ me that she was hungry.

2. Ava _____*said*_____ that she was hungry.

3. Ava _____ me if I wanted to go out to lunch with her.

4. When the storm began, I _____ the children to come

   into the house.

5. When I talked to Mr. Grant, he _____ he would be at the meeting.

6. Ali _____ his friends that he had won a scholarship to college. His friends

   _____ they weren't surprised.

7. My supervisor _____ me if I could postpone my vacation. I _____ him

   what the reason was. He _____ that our sales department needed me for a project.

8. My neighbor and I had a disagreement. I

   _____ my neighbor that he was wrong. My

   neighbor _____ me that I was wrong.

9. Fumiko _____ the teacher that Fatima wasn't

   going to be in class.

10. Ellen _____ if I could join her for a movie.

    I _____ I wasn't feeling well, but

    I _____ her what movie she was going to.

    The next day, Ellen _____ me she had enjoyed the movie.

▶ **Practice 25. Reported speech.** (Charts 14-1 → 14-10)

Complete the sentences by changing the quoted speech to reported speech. Use *said*, *told*, *asked*, or *replied*. Practice using the formal sequence of tenses.

1. Alex said, "Where do you live?"   Alex _____*asked me where I lived.*_____

2. He said, "Do you live in the dorm?"   He _____ in
                                           the dorm.

3. I said, "I have my own apartment."   I _____ my own
                                           apartment.

4. He said, "I'm looking for a new apartment."   He _____
                                           for a new apartment.

5. He said, "I don't like living in the dorm."   He _____ in
                                           the dorm.

6. I said, "Do you want to move in with me?"   I _____

7. He said, "Where is your apartment?"   He _____

8. I said, "I live on Seventh Avenue."   I _____
                                           on Seventh Avenue.

9. He said, "But I can't move   He _____
   until the end of May."   until the end of May.

10. He said, "I will cancel my dorm contract at   He _____
    the end of May."   dorm contract at the end of May.

11. He said, "Is that okay?"   He _____

12. I said, "I'm looking forward to having you   I _____
    as a roommate."   as a roommate.

▶ **Practice 26. Reported speech.** (Charts 14-1 → 14-10)

Check (✓) <u>all</u> the correct sentences.

1. _____ a. The teacher asked are you finished?
   _✓_ b. The teacher asked if I was finished.
   _____ c. The teacher asked if was I finished?
   _____ d. The teacher asked that I was finished?
   _✓_ e. The teacher asked, "Are you finished?"

2. _____ a. Aki said he was finished.
   _____ b. Aki said that he was finished.
   _____ c. Aki replied that he was finished.
   _____ d. Aki answered that he was finished.
   _____ e. Aki said whether was he finished.

3. _____ a. Ann told Tom, she needed more time.
   _____ b. Ann told Tom she needed more time.
   _____ c. Ann told to Tom she needed more time.
   _____ d. Ann told she needed more time.
   _____ e. Ann said Tom she needed more time.
   _____ f. Ann said she needed more time.

4. _____ a. Donna answered that she was ready.

 _____ b. Donna answered was she ready.

 _____ c. Donna replied ready.

 _____ d. Donna answered, "I am ready."

 _____ e. Donna answered if she was ready.

5. _____ a. Mr. Wong wanted to know if Ted was coming.

 _____ b. Mr. Wong wanted to know is Ted coming?

 _____ c. Mr. Wong wondered if Ted was coming.

 _____ d. Mr. Wong wondered was Ted coming.

 _____ e. Mr. Wong wondered, "Is Ted coming?"

▶ **Practice 27. Reported speech.** (Charts 14-1 → 14-10)
Part I. Read the fable by Aesop.*

The Ant and the Grasshopper

(1–2) In a field one summer's day, a grasshopper was jumping around
and thinking to himself, "It's a beautiful day, and I love playing in the sun."

(3) An ant passed by. The Ant was carrying a heavy piece of corn.

(4–5) The Grasshopper asked the Ant, "What are you doing and
where are you going?"

(6) The Ant replied, "I am carrying food to my nest."

(7–8) The Grasshopper asked "Why are you working so hard in the
beautiful weather?"

(9) The Ant said, "If I bring food to the nest in the summer, I can have food in the winter."

(10–11) The Grasshopper asked the Ant, "Can you take a break now and play with me instead
of working?"

(12) The Ant answered, "I can't."

(13–14) The Ant said, "If I don't bring food to the nests in the summer, I won't have any food
for the winter."

(15) The Grasshopper said, "I'm not worried about the winter because I have plenty of food."

(16–17) The Ant continued walking. The Grasshopper saw many ants doing the same thing.
They were carrying heavy loads of food on their backs, and they were all going back to their nests.

(18) The Grasshopper wondered, "Do those ants ever have any fun?"

(19–22) The Grasshopper continued to play in the beautiful weather, and he played all summer
long. When winter came, the Grasshopper had no food. In fact, he was getting hungrier and
hungrier. The Grasshopper saw the ants. They were eating all the corn and grain that they had
collected during the summer.

(23–24) Then the Grasshopper thought to himself, "The ants are smart because they prepared
for the winter."

(25–26) And just before the Grasshopper died, he said to himself, "It is always a good idea to
prepare for the future."

---

*A fable teaches a lesson about right or wrong. Aesop was a Greek writer who wrote many fables.

Part II. Complete the sentences by changing the quoted speech to indirect speech. Use formal sequence of tenses.

1. (Lines 1–2) The Grasshopper was thinking to himself _____*that it was a beautiful day, and*_____
   _____*he loved playing in the sun*_____ .

2. (Line 4) The Grasshopper asked the Ant _____*what he was doing*_____
   and _____.

3. (Line 6) The Ant replied _____
   _____.

4. (Lines 7–8) The Grasshopper asked the Ant _____
   _____.

5. (Line 9) The Ant said _____
   _____.

6. (Lines 10–11) The Grasshopper asked the Ant _____
   _____.

7. (Line 12) The Ant answered _____.

8. (Lines 13–14) The Ant said _____
   _____.

9. (Line 15) The Grasshopper said _____
   _____.

10. (Line 18) The Grasshopper wondered _____
    _____.

11. (Lines 23–24) The Grasshopper thought _____
    _____.

12. (Lines 25–26) The Grasshopper said _____
    _____.

▶ **Practice 28. Editing.** (Chapter 14)
Correct the errors.

1. Excuse me. May I ask if how old are you?

2. I wonder did Rashed pick up something for dinner?

3. I'm unsure what does Lawrence do for a living.

4. Fernando said, "the best time for me to meet would be Thursday morning.

5. Eriko said to me was I coming to the graduation party. I say her that I wasn't.

6. I hope so that I will do well on my final exams.

7. I'm not sure if that the price includes the sales tax or not.

8. My mother said to me that, "How many hours did you spend on your homework?"

9. I told my brother, "Are you going to marry Paula?"

10. I'd like to know how do you do that.

11. My parents knew what did Sam and I do.

12. Is a fact that unexpected things happen in everyone's lives.

▶ **Practice 29. Word search puzzle.** (Chapter 14).
Circle the words that are the past tense forms of verbs often used to introduce noun clauses in reported speech. There are seven words in the puzzle.

The words may be horizontal, vertical, or diagonal. The first letter of each word is highlighted in gray.

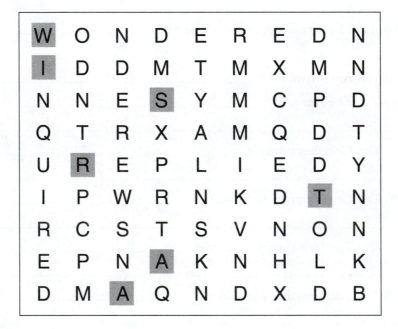

W	O	N	D	E	R	E	D	N
I	D	D	M	T	M	X	M	N
N	N	E	S	Y	M	C	P	D
Q	T	R	X	A	M	Q	D	T
U	R	E	P	L	I	E	D	Y
I	P	W	R	N	K	D	T	N
R	C	S	T	S	V	N	O	N
E	P	N	A	K	N	H	L	K
D	M	A	Q	N	D	X	D	B

Appendix 1
Phrasal Verbs

▶ **Practice 1. Group A.***
Complete the examples for the chart.

Group A: Phrasal Verbs (separable)		
Verb	**Definition**	**Example**
figure out	find the solution to a problem	I *figured* ___out___ the answer.
hand in	give homework, papers, etc., to a teacher	We *handed* _____ our homework.
hand out	give something to this person, then that person, etc.	The teacher *handed* _____ the test papers to the class.
look up	look for information in a dictionary, phone book, online, etc.	I *looked* a word _____ in the dictionary.
make up	invent (a story)	Children like to *make* _____ stories.
pick up	lift	Tom *picked* _____ the baby.
put down	stop holding or carrying	I *put* _____ the heavy packages.
put off	postpone	We *put* _____ our trip until next summer.
put on	place clothes on one's body	I *put* _____ my coat before I left.
take off	remove clothes from one's body	I *took* _____ my coat when I arrived.
throw away } . . . . put in the trash, discard **throw out**		I *threw* _____ my old notebooks. I *threw* _____ my old notebooks.
turn off	stop a machine or a light	I *turned* _____ the lights and went to bed.
turn on	start a machine or a light	I *turned* _____ the light so I could read.
wake up	stop sleeping	I *woke* _____ at six.
write down	write a note on a piece of paper	I *wrote* his phone number _____.

▶ **Practice 2. Group A**
Complete the sentences with particles from the list.

away	down	in	off	on	out	up

1. Johnny is all wet. I told him to take _____ his clothes and put _____ some dry ones.

2. Lilly made _____ a story. She didn't tell the truth.

*Appendix 1 presents phrasal verbs in small groups to be learned and practiced one group at a time. A complete reference list can found in the Student Book, pp. 399–400.

3. Alice used her online dictionary to look _____ a word. Then she wrote the definition _____.

4. Sometimes I postpone doing my homework. My parents get upset and tell me not to put it _____. They also get mad because I hand _____ some assignments late.

5. My arms hurt, so I put the baby _____ for a minute. But he started crying right away, so I picked him _____ again.

6. My roommate is messy. He never picks _____ his clothes.

7. My mother woke me _____ at 7:00, but I didn't get up until 7:30. I turned _____ the light and went back to sleep.

8. We don't need these receipts anymore. We can throw them _____.

9. When I got my physics test today, I realized that I couldn't figure _____ any of the answers. Our teacher had made a mistake and handed _____ the wrong test!

▶ **Practice 3. Group A.**
Choose all the correct completions for each sentence.

1. Akiko turned off   (the TV)   the butter   (the stove.)
2. I took off   my coat   my toys   my wedding ring.
3. Jonas put on   his shoes   a fire   the dishes.
4. Benjamin made up   a story   a fairy tale   an excuse.
5. Susanna threw out   some air   some rotten food   an old shirt.
6. Antonio put off   a doctor's appointment a meeting   a trip.
7. Max figured out   a puzzle   a math problem   difficult.
8. Kyong handed in   some candy   a report   some late homework.
9. The secretary wrote down   a message   a pencil   a phone number.
10. The mail carrier put down a box   the mail truck   a sack of mail.
11. Mustafa turned off   the light   the computer   the car engine.

▶ **Practice 4. Group B.**
Complete the examples for the chart.

Group B: Phrasal Verbs (nonseparable)		
Verb	**Definition**	**Example**
call on	ask (someone) to speak in class	The teacher *called* _____ Ali.
come from	originate	Where do these bananas *come* _____ ?
get over	recover from an illness or a shock	Sue *got* _____ her cold quickly.
get off	leave ⎫	I *got* _____ the bus at First Street.
get on	enter ⎭ a bus/airplane/train/subway	I *got* _____ the bus at Fifth Street.
get in/into	enter ⎫	I *got* _____ the taxi at the airport.
get out of	leave ⎭ a car, a taxi	I *got* _____ _____ the taxi at the hotel.
look into	investigate	The police are *looking* _____ the crime.
run into	meet by chance	I *ran* _____ Peter at the store.

▶ Practice 5. Group B.

Complete the sentences with particles from the list.

from	in	into	off	on	out of	over

1. When I raised my hand in class, the teacher called _____ me.

2. Fred feels okay today. He got _____ his cold.

3. Last week I flew from Chicago to Miami. I got _____ the plane in Chicago. I got _____ the plane in Miami.

4. Sally took a taxi to the airport. She got _____ the taxi in front of her apartment building. She got _____ the taxi at the airport.

5. I take the bus to school every day. I get _____ the bus at the corner of First Street and Sunset Boulevard. I get _____ the bus just a block away from the classroom building.

6. The receptionist at the power company didn't know why my bill was so high, but she said she would look _____ it.

7. I ran _____ Pierre at the mall. He's married and has ten kids!

▶ Practice 6. Group B.

Complete each sentence in Column A with the correct phrase from Column B.

Example: Annette speaks both French and English because she comes . . .
   Annette speaks both French and English because she comes from Quebec.

Column A

1. Annette speaks both French and English because she comes . . . .

2. When Sylvia lost her job, it took her several weeks to get . . . .

3. Our office will need several days to look . . . .

4. When a plane lands, the first-class passengers get . . . .

5. While I was walking in the mall, I ran . . . .

6. When he left the hotel, David got . . . .

7. Mrs. Riley, our math teacher, often calls . . . .

Column B

a. into your request for medical records.

✓b. from Quebec.

c. over the shock.

d. into a taxi and went to the airport.

e. on unprepared students.

f. into several friends from high school.

g. off first.

▶ **Practice 7. Group C.**
Complete the examples for the chart.

Group C: Phrasal Verbs (separable)		
Verb	**Definition**	**Example**
ask out	ask (someone) to go on a date	Tom *asked* Sue _____. They went to a movie.
call back	return a telephone call	I'll *call* you _____ tomorrow.
call off	cancel	We *called* _____ the picnic because of the rain.
call up	make a telephone call	I *called* _____ my friend in New York.
give back	return something to someone	I borrowed Al's pen, then I *gave* it _____.
hang up	hang on a hanger or a hook	I *hung* my coat _____ in the closet.
pay back	return borrowed money to someone	Thanks for the loan. I'll *pay* you _____ soon.
put away	put something in its usual or proper place	I *put* the clean dishes _____.
put back	return something to its original place	I *put* my books _____ into my bag.
put out	extinguish (stop) a fire, a cigarette	We *put* _____ the campfire before we left.
shut off	stop a machine or light, turn off	I *shut* _____ my printer before I left the office.
try on	put on clothing to see if it fits	I *tried* _____ several pairs of shoes.
turn down	decrease the volume	Sue *turned* _____ the music. It was too loud.
turn up	increase the volume	Al *turned* _____ the radio. He likes loud music.

▶ **Practice 8. Group C.**
Complete the sentences with particles from the list.

away	back	down	off	on	out	up

1. You still owe me the money I lent you. When are you going to pay me _____?

2. Turn _____ the radio! It's too loud! I can't hear myself think.

3. Debra put _____ the fire in the oven with a fire extinguisher.

4. I'll wash and dry the dishes, and you can put them _____.

5. Before you buy shoes, you should try them _____ to see if they fit.

6. I can't hear the TV. Could you please turn it _____?

7. You took my toy! Give it _____.

8. I didn't hear anyone on the other end of the phone, so I hung _____.

9. You can look at these books, but please put them _____ on the shelf when you're finished.

10. Bob hasn't paid his electric bill for months, so the electric company shut his power
_____.

11. A: I hear that Tom asked you _____ for next Saturday night.

    B: Yes, he did. He called me _____ a couple of hours ago and invited me to a
    dance.

    A: The dance has been called _____ because the musicians are on strike. Didn't
    you hear about it?

    B: No, I didn't. I'd better call Tom _____ and ask him what he wants to do instead.

▶ Practice 9. Phrasal verbs: separable. (Groups A, B, C)
Complete the sentences with a given particle where possible. If not possible, write "**X**."

1. *out*   a. Paulo asked _____*out*_____ one of his classmates.

           b. Paulo asked one of his classmates _____*out*_____.

2. *on*   a. The teacher called _____*on*_____ Ted for the answer.

           b. The teacher called Ted _____*X*_____ for the answer.

3. *into* a. The police are looking _____ the murder, but need help from the public
              to solve it.

           b. The police are looking the murder _____, but need help from the public
              to solve it.

4. *into* a. Khalifa ran his cousin _____ at the store.

           b. Khalifa ran _____ his cousin at the store.

5. *up*   a. Claire turned _____ the ringer on the phone.

           b. Claire turned the ringer on the phone _____.

6. *away* a. Dr. Benson threw _____ a valuable coin by mistake.

           b. Dr. Benson threw a valuable coin _____ by mistake.

7. *down* a. Yumi's baby cries whenever she puts him _____.

           b. Yumi's baby cries whenever she puts _____ him.

8. *up*   a. Would you please wake _____ me in one hour?

           b. Would you please wake me _____ in one hour?

9. *away* a. You can leave the dishes. I'll put them _____ later.

           b. You can leave the dishes. I'll put _____ them later.

10. *up*   a. When Joan feels lonely, she calls _____ a friend and talks for a while.

           b. When Joan feels lonely, she calls a friend _____ and talks for a while.

11. *off* a. The hill was so steep that I had to get _____ my bicycle and walk.

           b. The hill was so steep that I had to get my bicycle _____ and walk.

12. *from* a. This fruit is very fresh. It came _____ my garden.

           b. This fruit is very fresh. It came my garden _____.

► **Practice 10. Group D.**
Complete the examples.

Group D: Phrasal Verbs (separable)		
Verb	**Definition**	**Example**
cross out	draw a line through	I *crossed* _____ the misspelled word.
fill in	complete by writing in a blank space	We *fill* _____ blanks in grammar exercises.
fill out	write information on a form	I *filled* _____ a job application.
fill up	fill completely with gas, water, coffee, etc.	We *filled* _____ the gas tank.
find out	discover information	I *found* _____ where he lives.
have on	wear	She *has* a blue blouse _____.
look over	examine carefully	*Look* _____ your paper for errors before you hand it in.
point out	call attention to	The teacher *pointed* _____ a misspelling.
print out	create a paper copy from a computer	I finished the letter and *printed* it _____.
tear down	destroy a building	They *tore* _____ the old house and built a new one.
tear out (of)	remove (paper) by tearing	I *tore* a page _____ _____ a magazine.
tear up	tear into small pieces	I *tore* _____ the secret note.
turn around⎫ . . . . **turn back** ⎭	change to the opposite direction	After a mile, we *turned* _____/_____.
turn over	turn the top side to the bottom	I *turned* the paper _____ and wrote on the back.

► **Practice 11. Group D.**
Complete the sentences with particles from the list.

around	back	down	in	of	out	over	up

1. When I finish writing on one side of the paper, I turn it _____*over*_____ and write on the back.

2. When the teacher finds a mistake in our writing, she points it _____ so we can correct it.

3. When I write words in this practice, I am filling _____ the blanks.

4. When I discover new information, I find something _____.

5. When I need to see information from my computer on paper, I print it _____.

6. When buildings are old and dangerous, we tear them _____.

7. When I turn and go in the opposite direction, I turn _____.

8. When I remove a piece of paper from a spiral notebook, I tear the paper _____ _____ my notebook.

9. When I write something that I don't want anybody else to see, I tear the paper into tiny pieces. I tear _____ the paper.

10. When I write information on an application form, I fill the form _____.

11. When I make a mistake in something I write, I erase the mistake if I'm using a pencil. If I'm using a pen, I cross the mistake _____ by drawing a line through it.

12. When my juice glass is empty, I fill it _____ again if I'm still thirsty.

13. When I check my homework carefully before I give it to the teacher, I look it _____ .

▶ **Practice 12. Groups A, B, C, D**

Complete the sentences with the particles in *italics*. The particles may be used more than once or not at all.

1. *out, away, back, down, off, on*

Carol . . .

a. put _____off_____ her vacation because she was sick.

b. put _____ her boots to go out in the rain.

c. put the phone _____ when she saw a spider crawling toward her.

d. put her things _____ in her suitcase after the customs officer checked them.

e. put _____ the stovetop fire with a small fire extinguisher.

f. put _____ all the groceries she bought before she started dinner.

2. *out, in, up*

James . . .

a. handed _____ his financial report before the due date.

b. handed _____ thank-you gifts to his staff for their hard work.

3. *into, off, on, up, over, out of*

Linda . . .

a. got _____ the flu in three days and felt wonderful.

b. got _____ the bus and walked home.

c. got _____ the bus and sat down behind the driver.

d. got _____ a taxi to go to the airport.

e. got _____ the taxi, paid the driver, and left a nice tip.

4. *in, down, up, out*

a. This book has a few pages missing. The baby tore them _____ .

b. Before I throw my credit card receipts away, I tear them _____ . I don't want anyone to read them.

c. The building across the street will be torn _____ to make room for a parking garage.

5. *over, into, up*

a. The neighbors asked the sheriff to look _____ a crime in their neighborhood.

b. The sheriff looked _____ a suspect's address on the computer.

c. The sheriff took the suspect's ID, looked it _____ slowly, and decided it was fake.

6. *off, down, up, back*

   a. I called Rita _____ several times, but got no answer. I'm a little worried.

   b. The meeting was called _____ because the chairperson was sick.

   c. Jack called and left a message. I'll call him _____ after dinner.

7. *over, up, in, off, back*

   a. You can't do your homework with the music on. Please turn it _____.

   b. It's cold, and I'm tired. Let's turn _____ and go home.

   c. Could I turn _____ the TV? I can't hear the news.

   d. Joe, the meat needs to be cooked on the other side. Would you turn it _____, please?

8. *in, out, up*

   a. I forgot to fill _____ a couple of blanks on the test. I hope I passed.

   b. Can I take this application home and fill it _____? I don't have much time now.

   c. Jack carries a thermos bottle to work. He fills _____ his cup when he gets thirsty.

   d. Gas is expensive. It costs a lot to fill _____ my tank.

▶ **Practice 13. Group E.**
Complete the examples for the chart.

Group E: Phrasal Verbs (separable)		
Verb	**Definition**	**Example**
blow out	extinguish (a match, a candle)	He *blew* the candles _____.
bring back	return	She *brought* my books _____ to me.
bring up	(1) raise (children)	The Lees *brought* _____ six children.
	(2) mention, start to talk about	He *brought* the news _____ in conversation.
cheer up	make happier	The good news *cheered* me _____.
clean up	make neat and clean	I *cleaned* _____ my apartment.
give away	donate, get rid of by giving	I didn't sell my old bike. I *gave* it _____.
help out	assist (someone)	Could you please *help* me _____?
lay off	stop employment	The company *laid* _____ 100 workers.
leave on	(1) not turn off (a light, a machine)	Please *leave* the light _____. I can't see.
	(2) not take off (clothing)	I *left* my coat _____ during class.
take back	return	She *took* a book _____ to the library.
take out	invite out and pay	He *took* Mary _____. They went to a movie.
talk over	discuss	We *talked* the problem _____.
think over	consider	I *thought* the problem _____.
work out	solve	We *worked* the problem _____.

Complete the sentences with particles from the list.

away	back	off	on	out	over	up

1. It's pretty chilly in here. You might want to leave your jacket _____.

2. My father speaks with an Australian accent. He was brought _____ in Australia.

3. The Smiths have marriage problems but they are trying to work them _____.

   They talk them _____ as soon as they occur.

4. After I lit the candles, I blew _____ the match.

5. My roommate gives _____ his old clothes to homeless people. He tries to help them _____ as often as possible.

6. I took my elderly parents _____ to a restaurant for their anniversary. Then I cleaned _____ their house the next day for them.

7. These are bad economic times. Businesses are laying _____ hundreds of workers.

8. The store's return policy is that you can bring clothes _____ within two weeks if you have a receipt.

9. I'm meeting with my supervisor later today. I'm going to bring _____ the idea of a raise.

10. I won't be home until midnight, so please leave some lights _____.

11. When I'm sad, my friends try to cheer me _____.

12. Are you sure you want to change jobs? Do you want to think it _____ some more?

13. I hate to bring this problem _____, but we need to talk about it.

14. I can't sell this old table. I guess I'll give it _____. Someone will be able to use it.

15. My parents usually help me _____ when I'm having trouble paying my bills.

16. You can borrow my tools, but when you finish, be sure to put them _____.

► **Practice 15. Group F.**
Complete the examples for the chart.

Group F: Phrasal Verbs (intransitive)		
Verb	**Definition**	**Example**
break down	stop functioning properly	My car *broke* _____ on the highway.
break out	happen suddenly	War *broke* _____ between the two countries.
break up	separate, end a relationship	Ann and Tom *broke* _____.
come in	enter a room or building	May I *come* _____?
dress up	put on nice clothes	People usually *dress* _____ for weddings.
eat out	eat outside of one's home	Would you like to *eat* _____ tonight?
fall down	fall to the ground	I *fell* _____ and hurt myself.
get up	get out of bed in the morning	What time did you *get* _____ this morning?
give up	quit doing something or quit trying	I can't do it. I *give* _____.
go on	continue	Let's not stop. Let's *go* _____.
go out	not stay home	Jane *went* _____ with her friends last night.
hang up	end a telephone conversation	When we finished talking, I *hung* _____.
move in (to)	start living in a new home	Some people *moved* _____ next door to me.
move out (of)	stop living at a place	My roommate is *moving* _____.
show up	come, appear	Jack *showed* _____ late for the meeting.
sit back	put one's back against a chair back	*Sit* _____ and relax. I'll get you a drink.
sit down	go from standing to sitting	Please *sit* _____.
speak up	(1) speak louder (2) express one's opinion without fear	I can't hear you. You'll have to *speak* _____.
stand up	go from sitting to standing	I *stood* _____ and walked to the door.
start over	begin again	I lost count, so I *started* _____.
stay up	not go to bed	I *stayed* _____ late last night.
take off	ascend in an airplane	The plane *took* _____ 30 minutes late.

► **Practice 16. Group F.**
Complete the sentences with particles from the list.

back	down	in	off	on	out	over	up

1. The plane shook a little when it took _____. It made me nervous.

2. I'm afraid we can't hear you in the back of the room. Could you please speak _____?

3. The computer teacher was so confusing. I didn't learn a thing! I think I'll just start _____ with a new teacher next term.

4. I was late to work. The bus broke _____, and we had to wait for another.

5. Mrs. Taylor is in the hospital again. She fell _____ and broke her hip.

6. Tim and Ann aren't getting married. They had a fight and broke _____ last night.

7. Julian's at the doctor's. He broke _____ in a rash last night, and he doesn't know what it is.

8. I'm very nervous when I fly. I can't just sit _____ and relax.

9. Sometimes when I stand _____ too fast, I get dizzy.

10. Someone keeps calling and hanging _____. It's very annoying.

11. Sorry, I didn't mean to interrupt you. Please go _____.

12. A: Professor Wilson, do you have a minute?

    B: Sure. Come _____ and sit _____.

▶ **Practice 17. Group F.**
Complete the sentences with particles from the list.

into	of	out	up

1. *Lazy Leo . . .*

   a. broke ____up____ with his girlfriend because she didn't want to wash his clothes.

   b. stayed _____ all night and didn't come home until morning.

   c. showed _____ late for class without his homework.

   d. goes _____ with friends to parties on school nights.

   e. eats _____ at restaurants because he doesn't like to cook.

   f. moved _____ _____ his apartment without telling the manager.

2. *Serious Sally . . .*

   a. goes to bed very early. She never stays _____ past 9:00.

   b. gets _____ at 5:00 every morning.

   c. speaks _____ in class when no one will answer.

   d. dresses _____ for school.

   e. moved _____ an apartment next to the library.

   f. never gives _____ when she gets frustrated.

3. *Independent Inga . . .*

   a. moved _____ _____ her parents' house when she was 16 and moved _____ her own apartment.

   b. goes _____ by herself when her friends are busy.

   c. speaks _____ when she disagrees with someone.

► **Practice 18. Group G.**
Complete the examples for the chart.

Group G: Phrasal Verbs (three-word)		
Verb	**Definition**	**Example**
drop in (**on**)	visit without calling first or without an invitation	We *dropped* _____ _____ my aunt.
drop out (**of**)	stop attending (school)	Beth *dropped* _____ _____ graduate school.
fool around (**with**)	have fun while wasting time	My son likes to *fool* _____ _____ his friends on the weekends.
get along (**with**)	have a good relationship with	I *get* _____ well _____ my roommate.
get back (**from**)	return from (a trip)	When did you *get* _____ _____ Hawaii?
get through (**with**)	finish	I *got* _____ _____ my work before noon.
grow up (**in**)	become an adult	Anika *grew* _____ _____ Sweden.
look out (**for**)	be careful	*Look* _____ _____ that car!
run out (**of**)	finish the supply of (something)	We *ran* _____ _____ gas.
sign up (**for**)	put one's own name on a list	Did you *sign* _____ _____ the school trip?
watch out (**for**)	be careful	*Watch* _____ _____ that car!

► **Practice 19. Group G.**
Complete the phrasal verbs.

1. Look _____! There's a car coming! Look _____ _____ the truck too!

2. I grew up in New Zealand. Where did you grow _____?

3. If you want to be in the class, you have to sign _____ _____ it first.

4. I couldn't finish the examination. I ran _____ _____ time.

5. My cousin never does anything useful. He just fools _____ _____ his friends all day, wasting time.

6. Joe is really tired. He just got _____ _____ a 10-day mountain climbing trip.

7. Jack dropped _____ _____ school last week. His parents are upset.

8. Watch _____ _____ the truck! It has a loose wheel.

9. Joanne got _____ _____ her work early, so she's leaving for vacation today.

10. My neighbor likes to drop _____ _____ us during dinner. I think she's lonely.

11. A: I want to move to another dorm room.

    B: Why?

    A: I don't get _____ _____ my roommate. She's sloppy and plays loud music when I'm trying to study.

Complete each sentence with the correct word from the list.

assignment	✓gymnastics class	paint	snakes
cord	Hawaii	rocks	their neighbors

1. Martin signed up for a _____gymnastics class_____. It starts next week.

2. The Hansens get along well with _____. They even take vacations together.

3. I can't finish the living room walls because I've run out of _____.

4. The highway sign said to watch out for _____. They roll down the hills and sometimes hit cars.

5. As soon as I get through with this _____, we can go to lunch. I have just one more problem to figure out.

6. Don't fool around with that _____. You might get an electric shock.

7. You look very rested and relaxed. When did you get back from _____?

8. Look out for _____ on the path. They're not poisonous, but they might startle you.

► **Practice 21. Group H.**
Complete the examples.

Group H: Phrasal Verbs (three-word)		
Verb	**Definition**	**Example**
come along (with)	accompany	Do you want to *come* _____ _____ us?
come over (to)	visit the speaker's place	Some friends are *coming* _____ tonight.
cut out (of)	remove with scissors or knife	I *cut* an article _____ _____ today's paper.
find out (about)	discover information about	When did you *find* _____ _____ the problem?
get together (with)	join, meet	Let's *get* _____ after work today.
go back (to)	return to a place	I *went* _____ _____ work after my illness.
go over (to)	(1) approach	I *went* _____ _____ the window.
	(2) visit another's home	Let's *go* _____ _____ Jim's tonight.
hang around (with) ⎫ . . . . . spend time relaxing		John likes to *hang* _____ the coffee shop.
hang out (with) ⎭		Kids like to *hang* _____ _____ each other.
keep away (from)	not give to	*Keep* matches _____ _____ children.
set out (for)	begin a trip	We *set* _____ _____ the mountain at sunrise.
sit around (with)	sit and do nothing	Don't *sit* _____ all day. Do something!

► **Practice 22. Group H.**

Complete each sentence with <u>two</u> particles.

1. Before we consider buying a home in this area, we'd like to find ___*out*___ more ___*about*___ the schools.
2. The mountain climbers set _____ _____ the summit at dawn and reached it by lunchtime.
3. When my grandma was 65, she decided to go _____ _____ school and get a college degree.
4. Some teenagers like to hang _____ _____ friends at the mall, but the management doesn't approve.
5. Susie needs to keep _____ _____ the dog. She's allergic to the fur.
6. I'm going shopping. Do you want to come _____ _____ me?
7. I invited my class to come _____ _____ our beach house on Saturday.
8. Oh, no. Tommy cut several pictures _____ _____ his new storybook.
9. A: Did you go _____ _____ Brian's last night?
   B: No, he wasn't home, so I sat _____ my apartment _____ my cat.

► **Practice 23. Group H.**

Complete the sentences with particles that will give the same meanings as the <u>underlined</u> words.

1. I'd like to <u>get information</u> about the company. I want to find ___*out*___ ___*about*___ it before I apply for a job there.

2. The two brothers <u>began their</u> fishing <u>trip</u> to the lake before sunrise. They set _____ early because they wanted to be the first ones there.

3. What time is the supervisor <u>returning</u>? I'd like to talk to him when he gets _____.

4. Mark won't be home for dinner. He plans to <u>join</u> his co-workers for a party.
   They only get _____ once a year, so Mark is looking forward to it.

5. The dog was growling when the dog catcher <u>approached</u> him. The dog catcher went _____ _____ him very carefully.

► **Practice 24. Review: Appendix 1**

Choose the correct particle.

1. Professor Brown always calls ____ the students who sit in the back of the class to answer.
   a. on   b. off   c. out   d. back

2. Tommy takes other children's toys and doesn't want to give them ____.
   a. away   b. back   c. in   d. to

3. My computer printer isn't working. I can't print ____ any of my work.
   a. out   b. in   c. over   d. back

4. Bobby, let's take a few minutes and pick ____ the toys in your room. They're all over the floor.
   a. over   b. on   c. up   d. away

5. Not enough people signed up ____ the math class, so it had to be canceled.
   a. for   b. in   c. into   d. with

6. This cold has lasted too long. I feel like I'll never get _____ it.
       a. with   b. over   c. away   d. back

7. Aren't you going to try _____ these shoes before you buy them?
       a. in   b. of   c. up   d. on

8. Keep away _____ the stove! It's still hot.
       a. off   b. from   c. out   d. of

9. Look how nice Jenny's bedroom looks! She spent all morning cleaning it _____.
       a. over   b. back   c. up   d. away

10. Steven had problems early in his career, but he seems to have worked them _____.
        a. up   b. over   c. off   d. out

11. Do you have a fire extinguisher in your house to put _____ fires?
        a. off   b. out   c. back   d. down

12. It took Tim only 20 minutes to figure _____ the answer to the puzzle.
        a. on   b. in   c. up   d. out

13. Mr. Beem is very wealthy and generous. He wants to give _____ all his money before he dies.
        a. away   b. in   c. into   d. from

14. I cut your picture out _____ the newspaper today. Did you know you were going to be in it?
        a. in   b. off   c. of   d. from

15. Some friends came _____ last night. We talked and listened to music.
        a. over   b. about   c. into   d. from

16. This hike is pretty exhausting. I don't think I can go _____. I need to rest.
        a. out   b. in   c. to   d. on

17. There's a gas station. I'll wash the windows while you fill _____ the tank.
        a. on   b. in   c. up   d. out

18. A fight broke _____ among students after school. Fortunately, no one was injured.
        a. out   b. down   c. in   d. off

19. I'm sorry, but you wrote about the wrong topic. You'll need to start _____.
        a. over   b. to   c. with   d. back

20. Tim didn't finish college. He dropped _____ after two years.
        a. in   b. off   c. of   d. out

21. Mr. Robinson is happy to lend his adult children money as long as they pay it _____.
        a. up   b. back   c. down   d. for

Appendix 2
Preposition Combinations

▶ **Practice 1. Group A.***

Test yourself and practice the preposition combinations. Follow these steps:

(1) **Cover** the ANSWERS column with a piece of paper.
(2) Complete the SENTENCES.
(3) Then remove the paper and check your answers.
(4) Then **cover** both the ANSWERS and the SENTENCES to complete your own REFERENCE LIST.

(5) Again check your answers.

Preposition Combinations: Group A		
Answers	**Sentences**	**Reference List**
from	He was absent _____*from*_____ work.	**be absent** _____*from*_____ s.t.**
of	I'm afraid _____*of*_____ rats.	**be afraid** _____*of*_____ s.t./s.o.**
about	I'm angry _____*about*_____ it.	**be angry** _____ s.t.
at / with	I'm angry _____ you.	**be angry** _____ s.o.
about	I'm curious _____ many things.	**be curious** _____ s.t./s.o.
to	This is equal _____ that.	**be equal** _____ s.t./s.o.
with	I'm familiar _____ that book.	**be familiar** _____ s.t./s.o.
of	The room is full _____ people.	**be full** _____ (*people/things*)
for	I'm happy _____ you.	**be happy** _____ s.o.
about	I'm happy _____ your good luck	**be happy** _____ s.t.
to	He's kind _____ people and animals.	**be kind** _____ s.o.
to	She's always nice _____ me.	**be nice** _____ s.o.
to	Are you polite _____ strangers?	**be polite** _____ s.o.
for	I'm ready _____ my trip.	**be ready** _____ s.t.
for	She's thirsty _____ lemonade.	**be thirsty** _____ s.t.

**s.t. = "something"; s.o. = "someone"

---

*Appendix 2 presents preposition combinations in small groups to be learned and practiced one group at a time.

▶ Practice 2. Group A.

Match each phrase in Column A with a phrase in Column B. Use each phrase only once.

Column A

1. Our dog is afraid _b_.

2. The class is curious _____.

3. Mr. White is angry _____.

4. Several nurses have been absent _____.

5. After gardening all day, Helen was thirsty _____.

6. The workers are angry _____.

7. The baseball coach was happy _____.

8. The kitchen cupboard is full _____.

9. I'm not ready _____.

10. It's important to be kind _____.

Column B

a. about his team's win

✓b. of cats

c. for a glass of lemonade

d. for the start of school

e. from work due to illness

f. about the snake in the cage

g. to everyone

h. of canned foods

i. about their low pay

j. at his dog for chewing his slippers

▶ Practice 3. Group A.

Complete the sentences with prepositions.

1. Mr. Porter is nice _____ everyone.

2. One inch is equal _____ 2.54 centimeters.

3. Joe has good manners. He's always polite _____ everyone.

4. I'm not familiar _____ that book. Who wrote it?

5. Anna got a good job that pays well. I'm very happy _____ her.

6. Anna is very happy _____ getting a new job.

7. Jack's thermos bottle is full _____ coffee.

8. The workers were angry _____ the decrease in their pay.

9. Half the students were absent _____ class yesterday. There is a flu virus going around.

10. I'm not familiar _____ that movie. Who is in it?

11. Children ask "Why" a lot. They are curious _____ everything.

12. William has been afraid _____ spiders since he was a child.

▶ Practice 4. Group B.

The prepositions in the column on the left are the correct completions for the blanks. Follow the same steps you used for Group A on page 270.

Preposition Combinations: Group B		
Answers	**Sentences**	**Reference List**
for	I admire you _____ your honesty.	**admire** s.o. _____ s.t.
for	He applied _____ a job.	**apply** _____ s.t.
with	I argued _____ my husband.	**argue** _____ s.o.
about / over	We argued _____ money.	**argue** _____ s.t.
in	My parents believe _____ me.	**believe** _____ s.o./s.t.
from	I borrowed a book _____ Oscar.	**borrow** s.t. _____ s.o.
with	I discussed the problem _____ Jane.	**discuss** s.t. _____ s.o.
with	Please help me _____ this.	**help** s.o. _____ s.t.
to	I introduced Sam _____ Helen.	**introduce** s.o. _____ s.o./s.t.
at	I laughed _____ the joke.	**laugh** _____ s.t./s.o.
for	I'm leaving _____ Rome next week.	**leave** _____ (*a place*)
at	Don't stare _____ me.	**stare** _____ s.o./s.t.

▶ Practice 5. Group B.

Complete the sentences with prepositions.

1. I borrowed this dictionary _____ Pedro.

2. Could you please help me _____ these heavy suitcases?

3. Sue, I'd like to introduce you _____ Ed Jones.

4. You shouldn't stare _____ other people. It's not polite.

5. Do you believe _____ ghosts?

6. Are you laughing _____ my mistake?

7. I admire my father _____ his honesty and intelligence.

8. I argued _____ Elena _____ politics.

9. I discussed my educational plans _____ my parents.

10. I applied _____ admission to the university.

11. We're leaving _____ Cairo next week.

▶ Practice 6. Groups A and B.

Complete the sentences with prepositions.

1. Dan is always nice _____ everyone.

2. A: How long do you need to keep the Spanish book you borrowed _____ me?

   B: I'd like to keep it until I'm ready _____ the exam next week.

3. A: Why weren't you more polite _____ Alan's friend?

   B: Because he kept staring _____ me all evening. He made me nervous.

4. $\frac{5}{10}$ is equal _____ $\frac{1}{2}$.

5. You did a lot of shopping. The refrigerator is full _____ food.

6. May I please borrow some money _____ you? I'm thirsty _____ an ice cream soda, and we're walking right by the ice cream shop.

7. A: Mike, I really admire you _____ your ability to remember names. Will you help me _____ the introductions?

   B: Sure. Ellen, let me introduce you _____ Pat, Andy, Olga, and Ramon.

▶ Practice 7. Group C.

The prepositions in the column on the left are the correct completions for the blanks. Follow the same steps you used for Group A on page 270.

Preposition Combinations: Group C		
Answers	**Sentences**	**Reference List**
of	I'm aware _____ the problem.	**be aware** _____ s.t./s.o.
for	Smoking is bad _____ you.	**be bad** _____ s.o./s.t.
to	The solution is clear _____ me.	**be clear** _____ s.o
about	Alex is crazy _____ football.	**be crazy** _____ s.t.
from	Jane is very different _____ me.	**be different** _____ s.o./s.t.
for	Venice is famous _____ its canals.	**be famous** _____ s.t.
to / with	She's friendly _____ everyone.	**be friendly** _____ s.o.
for	Fresh fruit is good _____ you.	**be good** _____ s.o.
for	I'm hungry _____ some chocolate.	**be hungry** _____ s.t.
in	I'm interested _____ art.	**be interested** _____ s.t.
about	I'm nervous _____ my test scores.	**be nervous** _____ s.t.
with	I'm patient _____ children.	**be patient** _____ s.o.
of	My parents are proud _____ me.	**be proud** _____ s.o./s.t.
for	Who's responsible _____ this?	**be responsible** _____ s.t./s.o.
about	I'm sad _____ losing my job.	**be sad** _____ s.t.
to	A lemon is similar _____ a lime.	**be similar** _____ s.o./s.t.
of / about	I'm sure _____ the facts.	**be sure** _____ s.t.

▶ Practice 8. Group C.

Complete the sentences with prepositions.

1. I don't understand that sentence. It isn't clear _____ me.

2. Mark Twain is famous _____ his novels about life on the Mississippi River.

3. I'm hungry _____ some chocolate ice cream.

4. Our daughter graduated from the university. We're very proud _____ her.

5. A lot of sugar isn't good _____ you. It is bad _____ your teeth.

6. Who was responsible _____ the accident?

7. My coat is similar _____ yours, but different _____ Ben's.

8. Some people aren't friendly _____ strangers.

9. My daughter is crazy _____ horses. She is very interested _____ them.

10. Sara knows what she's talking about. She's sure _____ her facts.

Complete the sentences with prepositions.

1. Dr. Nelson, a heart specialist, is . . . .

    a. proud _____ her work.

    b. famous _____ her medical expertise.

    c. sure _____ her skills.

    d. familiar _____ the latest techniques.

    e. patient _____ her patients.

    f. aware _____ the stresses of her job.

    g. interested _____ her patients' lives.

    h. kind _____ her patients' families.

2. Her patient, Mrs. Green, is . . . .

    a. sad _____ her illness.

    b. nervous _____ an upcoming surgery.

    c. aware _____ her chances for survival.

    d. full _____ hope.

    e. not afraid _____ dying.

    f. curious _____ alternative medicines.

    g. ready _____ unexpected side effects.

    h. hungry _____ a home-cooked meal.

► **Practice 10. Group D.**

The prepositions in the column on the left are the correct completions for the blanks. Follow the same steps you used for Group A on page 270.

Preposition Combinations: Group D		
Answers	**Sentences**	**Reference List**
with	I agree _____ you.	**agree** _____ s.o.
about	I agree with you _____ that.	**agree with** s.o. _____ s.t.
in	We arrived _____ Toronto at six.	**arrive** _____ (*a city/country*)
at	We arrived _____ the hotel.	**arrive** _____ (*a building/room*)
about	We all complain _____ the weather.	**complain** _____ s.t./s.o.
of	A book consists _____ printed pages.	**consist** _____ s.t.
with	I disagree _____ you.	**disagree** _____ s.o.
about	I disagree with you _____ that.	**disagree with** s.o. _____ s.t.
from	She graduated _____ Reed College.	**graduate** _____ (*a place*)
to	Ted invited me _____ a picnic.	**invite** s.o. _____ s.t.
to	We listened _____ some music.	**listen** _____ s.t./s.o.
for	Jack paid _____ my dinner.	**pay** _____ s.t.
to	I talked _____ Lisa on the phone.	**talk** _____ s.o.
about	We talked _____ her problem.	**talk** _____ s.t.
on	A salesman waited _____ a customer.	**wait** _____ s.o.
for	We waited _____ the bus.	**wait** _____ s.t.
about	Sally complained to me _____ my dog.	**complain to** s.o. _____ s.t.

► Practice 11. Group D.

Complete the sentences with prepositions.

1. Tom paid _____ his airplane ticket in cash.

2. Joan graduated _____ high school two years ago.

3. I waited _____ the bus.

4. Jim is a waiter. He waits _____ customers at a restaurant.

5. I have a different opinion. I don't agree _____ you.

6. I arrived _____ this city last month.

7. I arrived _____ the airport around eight.

8. I listened _____ the news on TV last night.

9. The supervisor agreed _____ the employees' decision to work longer days and shorter weeks.

10. This practice consists _____ verbs that are followed by certain prepositions.

11. Jack invited me _____ his party.

12. I complained _____ the landlord _____ the leaky faucet in the kitchen.

13. Annie disagreed _____ her father _____ the amount of her weekly allowance.

14. Did you talk _____ Professor Adams _____ your grades?

► Practice 12. Groups A, B, and D.

Complete the sentences with prepositions.

1. Everyone is talking _____ the explosion in the high school chemistry lab.

2. Carlos was absent _____ class six times last term.

3. Fruit consists mostly _____ water.

4. Our children are very polite _____ adults.

5. Three centimeters is equal _____ approximately one and a half inches.

6. I borrowed some clothes _____ my best friend.

7. Are you familiar _____ ancient Greek history?

8. I discussed my problem _____ my uncle.

9. I admire you _____ your ability to laugh _____ yourself when you make a silly mistake.

10. A: Are you two arguing _____ each other _____ money again?

    B: Yeah, listen _____ this.

    A: Shhh. I don't want to hear any of this. Stop complaining _____ me _____ your finances. I don't agree with either of you.

▶ Practice 13. Group E.

The prepositions in the column on the left are the correct completions for the blanks. Follow the same steps you used for Group A on page 270.

Answers	Sentences	Reference List
about	She asked me _____ my trip.	**ask** s.o. _____ s.t. (inquire)
for	She asked me _____ my advice.	**ask** s.o. _____ s.t. (request)
to	This book belongs _____ me.	**belong** _____ s.o.
about / of	I dreamed _____ my girlfriend.	**dream** _____ s.o./s.t.
about	Do you know anything _____ jazz?	**know** _____ s.t.
at	I'm looking _____ this page.	**look** _____ s.t./s.o.
for	I'm looking _____ my lost keys.	**look** _____ s.t./s.o. (search)
like	Anna looks _____ her sister.	**look** _____ s.o. (resemble)
to	I'm looking forward _____ vacation.	**look forward** _____ s.t.
to	Your opinion doesn't matter _____ me.	**matter** _____ s.o.
with	Something is the matter _____ the cat.	**be the matter** _____ s.t./s.o.
for	I'm searching _____ my lost keys.	**search** _____ s.t./s.o.
from	She separated the boys _____ the girls.	**separate** (*this*) _____ (*that*)
about / of	I warned them _____ the danger.	**warn** s.o. _____ s.t.

▶ Practice 14. Group E.

Complete the sentences with prepositions.

1. What's the matter _____ Billy? Is he hurt?

2. We can go out for dinner, or we can eat at home. It doesn't matter _____ me.

3. To make this recipe, you have to separate the egg whites _____ the yolks.

4. I don't know anything _____ astrology.

5. I'm looking forward _____ my vacation next month.

6. Dennis dreamed _____ his girlfriend last night.

7. Right now I'm doing a practice. I'm looking _____ my book.

8. Jim can't find his book. He's looking _____ it.

9. Jim is searching _____ his book.

10. I asked the waitress _____ another cup of coffee.

11. I asked Rebecca _____ her trip to Japan.

12. Does this pen belong _____ you?

13. The city was warned _____ the hurricane in advance.

14. Do you think Jon looks _____ his father or his mother?

15. Magda is always looking _____ her keys. She seems pretty disorganized.

16. Look _____ those clouds. It's going to rain.

▶ Practice 15. Group E.

Make sentences by matching each phrase in Column A with a phrase in Column B. Use each phrase only once.

Column A

1. The sheriff is searching _____.

2. The baby keeps looking _____.

3. Once again, Rita is looking _____.

4. In this picture, Paula looks _____.

5. The Browns are looking forward _____.

6. Before you do the wash, you need to separate the darks _____.

7. Sometimes Joey is afraid to sleep. He often dreams _____.

8. Something's the matter _____.

9. The sign on the highway warned drivers _____.

10. We're planning to move here. Do you know much _____?

Column B

a. about monsters and dragons

b. to their 20th wedding anniversary

c. for her glasses. She always misplaces them

d. about the schools in this area

e. about high winds on the bridge

f. with this car. It's making strange noises

g. for the escaped prisoner

h. from the whites

i. at the TV screen. It has bright colors

j. like her mother. The resemblance is very strong

▶ Practice 16. Group F.

The prepositions in the column on the left are the correct completions for the blanks. Follow the same steps you used for Group A on page 270.

Answers	Sentences	Reference List
to	I apologized _____ my friend.	**apologize** _____ s.o.
for	I apologized _____ my behavior.	**apologize** _____ s.t.
of	I don't approve _____ Al's behavior.	**approve** _____ s.t.
to / with	I compared this book _____ that book.	**compare** (*this*) _____ (*that*)*
on	I depend _____ my family.	**depend** _____ s.o./s.t.
of / from	He died _____ heart disease.	**die** _____ s.t.
from	The teacher excused me _____ class.	**excuse** s.o. _____ s.t.
for	I excused him _____ his mistake.	**excuse** s.o. _____ s.t. (forgive)
for	I forgave him _____ his mistake.	**forgive** s.o. _____ s.t.
of	I got rid _____ my old clothes.	**get rid** _____ s.t./s.o.
to	What happened _____ your car?	**happen** _____ s.t./s.o.
on	I insist _____ the truth.	**insist** _____ s.t.
from	I protected my eyes _____ the sun.	**protect** s.t./s.o. _____ s.t./s.o.
on	I am relying _____ you to help me.	**rely** _____ s.o./s.t.
of	Mr. Lee took care _____ the problem.	**take care** _____ s.t./s.o.
for	Thank you _____ your help.	**thank** s.o. _____ s.t.

Preposition Combinations: Group F

*Also possible: *I compared this **and** that.* (***And*** is not a preposition. A parallel structure with **and** may follow **compare**.)

► Practice 17. Group F.

Complete the sentences with prepositions.

1. I apologized _____ Ann _____ stepping on her toe.

2. I thanked Sam _____ helping me fix my car.

3. My grandfather doesn't approve _____ gambling.

4. Please forgive me _____ forgetting your birthday.

5. My friend insisted _____ taking me to the airport.

6. Please excuse me _____ being late.

7. Children depend _____ their parents for love and support.

8. In my composition, I compared this city _____ my hometown.

9. Umbrellas protect people _____ rain.

10. We're relying _____ Jason to help us move into our new apartment.

11. We had mice in the house, so we set some traps to get rid _____ them.

12. Who is taking care _____ the children while you are gone?

13. What happened _____ your finger? Did you cut it?

14. My boss excused me _____ the meeting when I became ill.

15. What did Mr. Hill die _____?

► Practice 18. Group F.

Write "C" beside the correct sentences. Write "I" beside those that are incorrect. In some cases, both may be correct.

1. a. ___C___ John needs to be excused from the meeting.

   b. ___C___ John excused his co-worker for the accounting error.

2. a. ___C___ Do you approve of your government's international policies?

   b. ___I___ Do you approve on the new seat-belt law?

3. a. _____ I apologized for the car accident.

   b. _____ I apologized to Mary's parents.

4. a. _____ Why did you get rid over your truck? It was in great condition.

   b. _____ I got rid of several boxes of old magazines.

5. a. _____ Pierre died of a heart attack.

   b. _____ Pierre's father also died from heart problems.

6. a. _____ It's not a good idea to compare one student to another.

   b. _____ I wish my parents wouldn't compare me with my brother.

7. a. _____ We can rely on Lesley to keep a secret.

   b. _____ There are several people whom my elderly parents rely in for assistance.

8. a. _____ You can relax. I took care about your problem.

   b. _____ The nurses take wonderful care of their patients at Valley Hospital.

► **Practice 19. Group G.**
The prepositions in the column on the left are the correct completions for the blanks. Follow the same steps you used for Group A on page 270.

Preposition Combinations: Group G		
Answers	**Sentences**	**Reference List**
to	I'm accustomed _____ hot weather.	**be accustomed** _____ s.t.
to	I added a name _____ my address book.	**add** (*this*) _____ (*that*)
on	I'm concentrating _____ this Practice.	**concentrate** _____ s.t.
into	I divided the cookie _____ two pieces.	**divide** (*this*) _____ (*that*)
from	They escaped _____ prison.	**escape** _____ (*a place*)
about	I heard _____ the prison escape.	**hear** _____ s.t./s.o.
from	I heard about it _____ my cousin.	**hear about** s.t. _____ s.o.
from	The escapees hid _____ the police.	**hide** (s.t.) _____ s.o.
for	We're hoping _____ good weather.	**hope** _____ s.t.
by	I multiplied 8 _____ 2.	**multiply** (*this*) _____ (*that*)
to / with	I spoke _____ the teacher.	**speak** _____ s.o.
about	We spoke to Dr. Carter _____ my problem.	**speak to/with** _____ s.t.
about	I told the teacher _____ my problem.	**tell** s.o. _____ s.t.
from	I subtracted 7 _____ 16.	**subtract** (*this*) _____ (*that*)
about	I wonder _____ lots of curious things.	**wonder** _____ s.t.

► **Practice 20. Group G.**
Complete the sentences with prepositions.

1. Shhh. I'm trying to concentrate _____ this math problem.

2. How did the bank robbers escape _____ jail?

3. Did you tell your parents _____ the dent in their new car?

4. We're hoping _____ good weather tomorrow so we can go sailing.

5. Did you hear _____ the earthquake in Turkey?

6. I heard _____ my sister last week. She sent me an email.

7. I spoke _____ Dr. Rice _____ my problem.

8. I'm not accustomed _____ cold weather.

9. When you divide 6 _____ 2, the answer is 3.

10. When you subtract 1 _____ 6, the answer is 5.

11. When you multiply 6 _____ 3, the answer is 18.*

12. When you add 6 _____ 4, the answer is 10.**

13. George wondered _____ his team's chances of winning the tennis tournament.

14. Sally hid her journal _____ her younger sister.

---

*Also possible: *multiply 6 **times** 3*

Also possible: add 6 **and 4; add 6 **plus** 4

▶ Practice 21. Groups E, F, and G.

Complete the sentences with prepositions.

1. My father insisted _____ knowing the truth.

2. I was wondering _____ your birthday. What do you want to do?

3. What's the matter _____ you today?

4. He hid the money _____ his wife.

5. We separated the younger kids _____ the teenagers.

6. I apologized _____ my boss _____ my mistake.

7. We got rid _____ the insects in our apartment.

8. Who does this book belong _____?

9. The prisoners escaped _____ their guards.

10. Does it matter _____ you what time I call this evening?

11. We're looking forward _____ your visit.

12. Fresh vegetables are good _____ you.

13. Parents protect their children _____ harm.

14. Shhh. I'm trying to concentrate _____ my work.

15. I rely _____ my friends for their help.

16. I don't approve _____ Bob's lifestyle.

17. The official warned us _____ the danger of traveling in the countryside alone.

▶ Practice 22. Review: Appendix 2.

Choose the correct preposition.

1. What time do you need to be ready ____ work?
   a. at   b. about   c. on   d. for

2. One pound is equal ____ 2.2 kilos.
   a. for   b. to   c. in   d. on

3. Too many vitamins may be bad ____ your health.
   a. in   b. about   c. for   d. with

4. That box looks very heavy. Can I help you ____ it?
   a. with   b. in   c. about   d. on

5. Our cat got rid ____ all the mice in our basement.
   a. about   b. off   c. in   d. of

6. Everyone admires Mr. Kim ____ his generosity with his time and money.
   a. for   b. from   c. with   d. about

7. What happened ____ your hand? It's swollen.
   a. on   b. to   c. in   d. about

8. Paul is so smart. He graduated ____ the university in just three years.
   a. of   b. at   c. from   d. to

9. Angela has applied ____ several jobs in the airline industry, but she hasn't gotten an interview yet.
   a. to   b. with   c. of   d. for

10. This car can't belong _____ Mike. It's too nice!
    a. about   b. with   c. to   d. at

11. Monica loves vegetables, but she's not crazy _____ fruit.
    a. over   b. in   c. at   d. about

12. Jack paid _____ my dinner.
    a. with   b. for   c. on   d. in

13. I tried to tell Jessica _____ my trip, but she didn't seem interested. I wonder if she was jealous.
    a. to   b. about   c. with   d. off

14. We're really happy _____ Professor James. He just received an award for excellence in
    teaching.
    a. for   b. to   c. over   d. in

15. People say I shouldn't care what other students think, but their opinions matter _____ me.
    a. on   b. for   c. with   d. to

16. Annie eats vegetables only if they are separated _____ the other foods on her plate.
    a. between   b. from   c. with   d. to

17. Kristi forgave her twin sister _____ taking her cell phone without asking.
    a. about   b. from   c. for   d. with

18. Doctors say that even ten minutes of exercise a day is good _____ you.
    a. at   b. for   c. with   d. about

19. I'm sorry. Your explanation still isn't clear _____ me.
    a. to   b. with   c. about   d. in

20. My sister complained _____ the manager.
    a. for   b. with   c. at   d. to

21. She complained _____ the slow service in the restaurant.
    a. about   b. for   c. over   d. by

22. The problem with your answer is that you multiplied six _____ eight instead of subtracting it.
    a. to   b. from   c. by   d. over

Index

Answer Key

CHAPTER 8: CONNECTING IDEAS

PRACTICE 1, p. 133

1. My kitchen has a new <u>sink</u>, <u>refrigerator</u>, and <u>oven</u>.
    noun + noun + noun *(above sentence 1)*

2. Danny is a <u>bright</u> and <u>happy</u> child.
    adjective + adjective *(above sentence 2)*

3. I <u>picked</u> up the telephone and <u>dialed</u> Steve's number.
    verb + verb *(above sentence 3)*

4. I have a <u>computer</u>, a <u>printer</u>, and a <u>scanner</u> in my home office.
    noun + noun + noun *(above sentence 4)*

5. The cook <u>washed</u> the vegetables and <u>put</u> them in boiling water.
    verb + verb *(above sentence 5)*

6. My feet were <u>cold</u> and <u>wet</u>.
    adj. + adj. *(above sentence 6)*

7. Anita is <u>responsible</u>, <u>considerate</u>, and <u>trustworthy</u>.
    adj. + adj. + adj. *(above sentence 7)*

8. The three largest land animals are the <u>elephant</u>, the <u>rhinoceros</u>, and the <u>hippopotamus</u>.
    noun + noun + noun *(above sentence 8)*

9. A hippopotamus <u>rests</u> in water during the day and <u>feeds</u> on land at night.
    verb + verb *(above sentence 9)*

PRACTICE 2, p. 134

1. Birds fly, and fish swim. *(S V S V)*
2. Birds fly. Fish swim. *(S V S V)*
3. Dogs bark. Lions roar. *(S V S V)*
4. Dogs bark, and lions roar. *(S V S V)*
5. A week has seven days. A year has 365 days. *(S V S V)*
6. A week has seven days, and a year has 365 days. *(S V S V)*
7. Ahmed raised his hand, and the teacher pointed at him. *(S V S V)*
8. Ahmed raised his hand. The teacher pointed at him. *(S V S V)*

PRACTICE 3, p. 134

1. No change.
2. I opened the door, walked into the room, and sat down at my desk.
3. No change.
4. Their flag is green, black, and yellow.
5. No change.
6. Tom made a sandwich, poured a glass of juice, and sat down to eat his lunch.
7. Ms. Parker is intelligent, friendly, and kind.
8. No change.
9. Did you bring copies of the annual report for Sue, Dan, Joe, and Mary?
10. No change.
11. Can you watch television, listen to the radio, and read the newspaper at the same time?

PRACTICE 4, p. 134

1. I Amy jogged along the road. I road my bicycle.
2. C
3. C
4. I My mother trained our dog to get the newspaper. My father trained it to bark at strangers.
5. I The river rose. It flooded the towns in the valley.
6. C
7. C
8. C
9. I Sharon's children don't believe in astrology. They dismiss the information she gives them.

PRACTICE 5, p. 135

Answers may vary.
1. The twins' first names mean **silver** and **gold**.
2. In Japan, many people **live** a long time and **receive** respect when they are old.
3. The twins were **old** and **healthy**.
4. The twins **often** laughed and smiled.
5. The twins **always** had a simple lifestyle and always **walked** everywhere.
6. They **enjoyed** people, and they **enjoyed** each other.
7. Kin and Gin **had many** children **and** grandchildren.
8. When they died, Kin and Gin **weren't** together.

PRACTICE 6, p. 136

1. I talked to Amy for a long time, but she didn't listen.
2. No change.
3. No change.
4. No change.
5. Please call Jane, Ted, or Anna.
6. Please call Jane, Ted, and Anna.
7. No change.
8. I didn't call Leo, Sarah, or Hugo.
9. I waved at my friend, but she didn't see me.
10. I waved at my friend, and she waved back.

PRACTICE 7, p. 136

1.	a	5.	e
2.	d	6.	f
3.	g	7.	b
4.	h	8.	c

PRACTICE 8, p. 136

1.	c	5.	b
2.	b	6.	c
3.	a	7.	a
4.	c	8.	c

PRACTICE 9, p. 137

1. C
2. C
3. C
4. I I bought some apples, peaches, and bananas.
5. I I was hungry, so I ate an apple.
6. C
7. C
8. I My daughter is affectionate, shy, independent, and smart.

PRACTICE 10, p. 137

1. James has a cold. **He** needs to rest and drink plenty of fluids, so he should go to bed and drink water, fruit juices, or soda pop. **He** needs to sleep a lot, so he shouldn't drink fluids with caffeine, such as tea or coffee.
2. The normal pulse for an adult is between 60 and 80 beats per minute, but exercise, nervousness, excitement, and a fever will all make a pulse beat faster. **The** normal pulse for a child is around 80 to 90.
3. Edward Fox was a park ranger for 35 years. **During** that time, he was hit by lightning eight times. **The** lightning never killed him, but it severely burned his skin and damaged his hearing.

PRACTICE 11, p. 137

Gina wants a job as an air traffic controller. Every air traffic controller worldwide uses English, so it is important for her to become fluent in the language. She has decided to take some intensive English courses at a private language institute, but she isn't sure which one to attend. There are many schools available, and they offer many different kinds of classes. She has also heard of air traffic control schools that include English as part of their coursework, but she needs to have a fairly high level of English to attend. She has to decide soon, or the classes will be full. She's planning to visit her top three choices this summer and decide on the best one for her.

PRACTICE 12, p. 138

1. did
2. does
3. didn't
4. do
5. wasn't
6. is
7. will
8. am
9. won't
10. has
11. don't
12. doesn't

PRACTICE 13, p. 138

1.	does	7.	would
2.	doesn't	8.	does
3.	isn't	9.	can't
4.	are	10.	is
5.	will	11.	does
6.	can	12.	did

PRACTICE 14, p. 138

1. does Tom
   Tom does
2. does Brian
   Brian doesn't
3. was I
   I was
4. did Jean
   Jean did
5. did Jason
   Jason didn't
6. can Rick
   Rick can't
7. does Laura
   Laura does
8. does Alice
   Alice doesn't

PRACTICE 15, p. 139

Part I
1. can't either
2. doesn't either
3. did too
4. did too
5. couldn't either
6. would too

Part II
7. so is
8. neither did
9. neither is
10. neither have
11. so did
12. so does

PRACTICE 16, p. 139

1.	h	5.	g
2.	c	6.	d
3.	b	7.	a
4.	f	8.	e

PRACTICE 17, p. 140

1. Because his coffee was cold, Jack didn't finish it. **He** left it on the table and walked away.
2. I opened the window because the room was hot. **A** nice breeze came in.
3. Because the weather was bad, we canceled our trip into the city. **We** stayed home and watched TV.
4. Debbie loves gymnastics. **Because** she hopes to be on an Olympic team, she practices hard every day.
5. Francisco is very good in math. **Because** several colleges want him to attend, they are offering him full scholarships.

PRACTICE 18, p. 140

1. *lose weight*—Eric went on a diet because he wanted to lose weight.
2. *didn't have money*—The family couldn't buy food because they didn't have money.
3. *have several children*—Our neighbors are very busy because they have several children.
4. *be tired*—Because I am tired, I am going to bed.
5. *exercise every day*—Because Susan exercises every day, she is in great shape.
6. *have a high fever*—Because Jennifer has a high fever, she is going to the doctor.

PRACTICE 19, p. 140

1. a. He was hungry**, so** he ate a sandwich.
   b. **Because** he was hungry**,** he ate a sandwich.
   c. He ate a sandwich **because** he was hungry.
2. a. **Because** my sister was tired**,** she went to bed.
   b. My sister went to bed **because** she was tired.
   c. My sister was tired**, so** she went to bed.
3. a. Schoolchildren can usually identify Italy easily on a world map **because** it is shaped like a boot.
   b. **Because** Italy has the distinctive shape of a boot**,** schoolchildren can usually identify it easily.
   c. Italy has the distinctive shape of a boot**, so** schoolchildren can usually identify it easily on a map.

PRACTICE 20, p. 141

1. like
2. don't like
3. is
4. stayed
5. didn't change
6. didn't pass
7. ate
8. were

PRACTICE 21, p. 142

1. b
2. a
3. a
4. b
5. a
6. a
7. b
8. b

PRACTICE 22, p. 142

1. because
2. even though
3. even though
4. even though
5. because
6. Even though
7. Because
8. Because
9. Even though

PRACTICE 23, p. 143

1. because
2. because
3. although
4. Because
5. Although
6. although
7. because

PRACTICE 24, p. 144

1. c
2. a
3. c
4. b
5. b
6. c
7. b
8. b
9. a
10. c

PRACTICE 25, p. 145

1. I don't drink coffee, and my roommate **doesn't** either.
2. The flight was overbooked, **so** I had to fly on another airline. OR **Because** the flight was overbooked, I had to fly on another airline.
3. Many people use computers for email**,** the Internet, and word processing.
4. Even **though** my father works two jobs, he always has time to play soccer or baseball on weekends with his family.
5. I saw a bad accident**,** and my sister **did** too.
6. Oscar always pays his bills on time**,** but his brother **doesn't**.
7. **Although / Even though** my mother is afraid of heights, I took her up to the observation deck at the top of the building. OR Because . . . I **didn't take** her . . .
8. Janey doesn't like to get up early, and **Joe doesn't either / neither does Joe**.
9. My mother and my father **immigrated** to this country 30 years ago.
10. **Because** Maya is very intelligent, her parents want to put her in an advanced program at school.

PRACTICE 26, p. 146

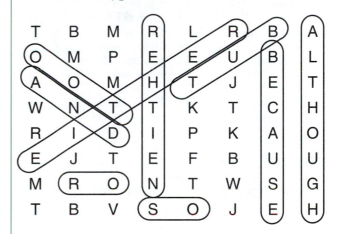

CHAPTER 9: COMPARISONS

PRACTICE 1, p. 147

1. (just) as busy as Jason (is).
2. (nearly) as busy as Jason (is)
3. (nearly) as tired as Susan (was).
4. (nearly) as tired as Susan (was).
5. (just) as lazy as her sister Amanda (is)
6. (nearly) as lazy as Alan (is)

PRACTICE 2, p. 147

1. aren't as strong as
2. is as tall as
3. isn't as wealthy as
4. isn't as polluted as
5. isn't as studious as
6. aren't as difficult as

PRACTICE 3, p. 148

Part I
1. not nearly as
2. almost as / not quite as
3. not nearly as
4. just as

Part II
5. just as
6. not nearly as
7. almost as / not quite as
8. not nearly as

Part III
9. just as
10. not nearly as
11. almost as / not quite as

Part IV
12. just as
13. almost as
14. just as
15. not nearly as
16. almost as / not quite as

PRACTICE 4, p. 149

Part I
1. as snow
2. as ice
3. as a picture
4. as a bat
5. as a bone
6. as a pillow
7. as a wink
8. as a mouse
9. as a bird
10. as pie

Part II
11. cold as ice
12. quick as a wink
13. blind as a bat
14. white as snow
15. quiet as a mouse
16. pretty as a picture
17. easy as pie
18. free as a bird
19. soft as a pillow
20. dry as a bone

PRACTICE 5, p. 150

1. stronger . . . the strongest
2. more important . . . the most important
3. softer . . . the softest
4. lazier . . . the laziest
5. more wonderful . . . the most wonderful
6. calmer . . . the calmest
7. tamer . . . the tamest
8. dimmer . . . the dimmest
9. more convenient . . . the most convenient
10. more clever / cleverer . . . the most clever / the cleverest
11. better . . . the best
12. worse . . . the worst
13. farther / further . . . the farthest / the furthest
14. slower . . . the slowest
15. more slowly . . . the most slowly

PRACTICE 6, p. 151

1. older than
2. more expensive than
3. larger
4. hotter than
5. slower than
6. creamier than
7. worse than
8. faster than
9. more important
10. quicker than
11. heavier
12. safer than
13. more difficult than

PRACTICE 7, p. 151

1. colder than . . . higher
2. foggier . . . sunnier
3. drier . . . healthier
4. more international . . .
   more expensive . . . cheaper

PRACTICE 8, p. 152

1. prettier
2. more careful
3. more energetic
4. more comfortable
5. more generous
6. richer
7. quietly . . . quiet
8. quiet . . . noisier . . . more noisily . . . more noisily . . .
   more noisily

PRACTICE 9, p. 153

1. the worst
2. worse
3. the best
4. better
5. the worst
6. worse
7. the worst
8. better

PRACTICE 10, p. 153

1. a, b
2. b
3. a, b
4. b
5. b
6. a, b

PRACTICE 11, p. 153

1. more slowly (adv)
2. slower (adj)
3. more serious (adj)
4. more seriously (adv)
5. more politely (adv)
6. more polite (adj)
7. more careful (adj)
8. more carefully (adv)
9. more clearly (adv)
10. clearer (adj)

PRACTICE 12, p. 154

1. I did / me
2. she is / her
3. she did / her
4. I was / me
5. he will / him
6. he has / him
7. I am / me
8. he is / him
9. I am / me
10. she is / her

PRACTICE 13, p. 155

1. a
2. b, c, d
3. a
4. b, c, d
5. b, c, d
6. a
7. b, c, d
8. a
9. b, c, d

PRACTICE 14, p. 155

2. not as friendly as → less friendly than
   not as interesting as → less interesting than
   not as difficult → less difficult
3. not as convenient as → less convenient than
   not as close . . . as (No change.)
   not as exciting as → less exciting than
4. not as comfortable . . . as → less comfortable . . . than
   not as unhappy as → less unhappy than
   not as bad as (No change.)

4 ANSWER KEY Chapter 9

PRACTICE 15, p. 156

1. a, b, c
2. a, c
3. a, b, c
4. b, c
5. a, b
6. a

PRACTICE 16, p. 157

1. Sam enjoys football more than his best friend **does**.
2. No change.
3. The coach helped Anna more than Nancy **did**. OR The coach helped Anna more than **she / he helped** Nancy.
4. Sara likes tennis more than her husband **does**.
5. No change.
6. No change.
7. Charles knows Judy better than Kevin **does**. OR Charles knows Judy better than **he knows** Kevin.

PRACTICE 17, p. 157

1. more books
2. more enjoyment
3. more news
4. more readers
5. more cell phones
6. more things

PRACTICE 18, p. 158

Part I. Adjectives
1. more pleasant
2. louder
3. more difficult

Part II. Adverbs
4. more clearly
5. more carefully
6. faster

Part III. Nouns
7. more homework
8. more snow
9. more friends
10. more problems
11. more cars
12. more money

PRACTICE 19, p. 159

1. better and better
2. bigger and bigger
3. warmer and warmer
4. noisier and noisier
5. madder and madder
6. longer and longer
7. more and more expensive
8. friendlier and friendlier / more and more friendly
9. worse and worse

PRACTICE 20, p. 159

1. more . . . stronger
2. softer . . . easier
3. simpler . . . more relaxed
4. longer . . . more tired
5. harder . . . more

PRACTICE 21, p. 160

1. more she talked, the more excited she got
2. more he talked, the hungrier I got
3. the older you are, the more you understand
4. faster he talked, the more confused I became
5. the more the fans clapped and cheered, the better their team played

PRACTICE 22, p. 160

1. the tallest mountain
2. the biggest organ
3. the most common word
4. the farthest planet
5. The most popular sport
6. the most intelligent animals
7. the worst flood . . . the highest level
8. the best policy

PRACTICE 23, p. 161

Part I
1. the most difficult . . . ever
2. the easiest . . . ever
3. the most interesting . . . in
4. the best . . . of
5. the wisest . . . ever
6. the fastest . . . of
7. the most artistic of
8. the most brilliant . . . in
9. the most successful . . . in
10. the busiest . . . in
11. the most generous . . . ever
12. the most important . . . in

Part II
13. the least ambitious of
14. the least expensive . . . ever
15. the least populated . . . in
16. the least anxious . . . ever

PRACTICE 24, p. 162

Part I
1. A pencil . . . a phone
2. A diamond ring . . . a paper clip
3. A cup of coffee . . . a bag of coffee beans
4. Radios . . . MP3 players . . . big screen TVs
5. A compact car . . . a house
6. Footballs, soccer balls, . . . basketballs . . . table-tennis balls

Part II
7. Angel Falls . . . than Niagara Falls
8. Giessbach Falls . . . as Cuquenán Falls
9. Angel Falls . . . of all
10. Niagara Falls . . . as Angel Falls
11. Giessbach Falls . . . as Cuquenán Falls

Part III
12. Air . . . than iron
13. Iron . . . than wood
14. iron . . . of all
15. Air . . . as water
16. air . . . of all
17. Water . . . as air
18. Water . . . iron . . . than wood

PRACTICE 25, p. 163

1. a
2. b
3. b
4. a
5. a
6. b
7. a
8. b

PRACTICE 26, p. 164

1. the funniest . . . funnier
2. sadder . . . the saddest

3. the best . . . better
4. more exhausting . . . the most exhausting
5. happier . . . the happiest
6. more entertaining . . . the most entertaining
7. harder . . . the hardest
8. hotter . . . the hottest

PRACTICE 27, p. 164

1. c
2. c
3. c
4. a
5. b
6. a
7. b
8. c
9. a
10. c

PRACTICE 28, p. 165

1. more intelligent than . . . the smartest . . . in
2. the most popular . . . in
3. smaller than
4. More potatoes . . . than
5. the closest . . . faster than
6. the largest . . . in . . . the smallest . . . of
7. more information
8. kinder . . . more generous
9. more honest . . . than
10. the worst
11. the safest
12. faster . . . than
13. bigger than

PRACTICE 29, p. 166

1. alike
2. like
3. alike
4. alike
5. like
6. like
7. alike
8. like
9. like
10. alike

PRACTICE 30, p. 166

1. different from
2. similar to
3. the same as
4. different from
5. the same as
6. similar to
7. the same as
8. the same as
9. different from
10. similar to
11. different from

PRACTICE 31, p. 167

Part I
1. A is like D.
2. A and D are alike.
3. C is similar to A and D.
4. B is different from A, C, and D.

Part II
5. similar to
6. the same as
7. different
8. the same as
9. different from

PRACTICE 32, p. 167

1. like
2. like
3. alike
4. A: alike
   B: the same . . . the same . . . the same
5. like

6. A: like
   B: similar
7. alike . . . alike . . . different
8. the same . . . the same . . . different

PRACTICE 33, p. 168

1. My brother is older **than** me.
2. A sea is **deeper** than a lake.
3. A donkey isn't as big **as** a horse.
4. Ellen is **the** happiest person I've ever met.
5. When I feel embarrassed, my face gets **hotter and hotter**.
6. One of **the** largest **animals** in the world is the hippopotamus.
7. The traffic on the highway is **worse** than it used to be.
8. Jack is the same **age as** Jerry / **as old as** Jerry.
9. Peas are similar **to** beans, but they have several differences.
10. Last winter was pretty mild. This winter is cold and rainy. It's much **rainier** than last winter.
11. Mrs. Peters, the substitute teacher, is **friendlier** than the regular instructor.
12. Although alligators and crocodiles are similar, alligators are **not as big as** / **smaller than** crocodiles.
13. Mohammed and Tarek come from different countries, but they became friends easily because they speak **the** same language, Arabic.

PRACTICE 34, p. 169

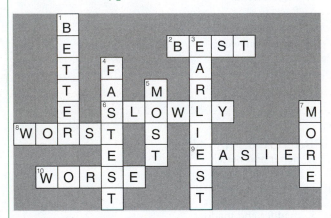

CHAPTER 10: THE PASSIVE

PRACTICE 1, p. 170

1. active, grow
2. passive, is grown
3. active, wrote
4. passive, was written
5. active, explained
6. passive, was explained
7. passive, are designed
8. active, design
9. active, are fixing
10. passive, is being fixed

PRACTICE 2, p. 170

1. is delivered
2. is being delivered
3. has been delivered
4. was delivered
5. was being delivered
6. is going to be delivered
7. will be delivered

PRACTICE 3, p. 171

Present		Present perfect	
1. c		13. p	
2. a		14. n	
3. b		15. m	
4. d		16. o	

Past		Progressive	
5. e		17. r	
6. g		18. q	
7. h		19. s	
8. f		20. t	

Future
9. k
10. i
11. l
12. j

PRACTICE 4, p. 172

1. brought		11. hit		20. saved	
2. built		12. hurt		21. sent	
3. bought		13. left		22. spoken	
4. carried		14. lost		23. spent	
5. done		15. made		24. taken	
6. eaten		16. planned		25. taught	
7. found		17. played		26. visited	
8. given		18. pulled		27. worn	
9. gone		19. read		28. written	
10. grown					

PRACTICE 5, p. 172

1. is spoken
2. are written
3. are read
4. was built
5. were found
6. has been eaten
7. is going to be visited
8. will be played
9. are going to be taken
10. have been grown
11. are being worn
12. was being carried

PRACTICE 6, p. 173

Part I
1. are collected
2. are written
3. is grown
4. are eaten
5. am paid
6. is understood

Part II
7. were collected
8. was built
9. were written
10. was destroyed

Part III
11. have been visited
12. has been spoken
13. has been read
14. has been worn

Part IV
15. will be discovered
16. will be visited
17. will be saved

Part V
18. is going to be hurt
19. are going to be offered
20. is going to be chosen

Part VI
21. is being announced
22. are being covered
23. am being treated
24. was being followed
25. were being washed

PRACTICE 7, p. 175

1. a		5. b	
2. b		6. a	
3. b		7. b	
4. a			

PRACTICE 8, p. 175

1. Was the game seen by many people?
2. Will Pat be shocked by the news?
3. Is lunch being served by the restaurant now?
4. Are the rules understood by everyone?
5. Is the solution going to be explained by the professor?
6. Have you been accepted by the university?
7. Has the contract been signed by both the buyer and the seller?
8. Was the thief found by the police?

PRACTICE 9, p. 176

1. collect taxes
2. use the tax money
3. provides many services
4. use these services
5. build and repair roads
6. train police forces
7. operates the fire department
8. pays teachers
9. issues professional licenses
10. runs the postal system
11. maintain armies
12. manage health care

PRACTICE 10, p. 176

1. The City Film Society will show a new film from India, *Falling Rocks*.
2. Movie critics have reviewed the film.
3. Audiences gave the movie good ratings.
4. Did a famous writer write the movie?
5. A new actress plays the main female part.
6. Does someone commit a murder in the movie?
7. Does a spy kill the main character?
8. Will many people see the movie?
9. Is the movie going to win an award?

PRACTICE 11, p. 177

1. transitive		letter
2. intransitive		No object.
3. intransitive		No object.
4. intransitive		No object.
5. transitive		the ball
6. intransitive		No object.
7. intransitive		No object.
8. transitive		the vase
9. transitive		the book
10. intransitive		No object.

PRACTICE 12, p. 177

1. No change.
2. me; I was awakened by loud sounds around midnight.
3. a tree; A tree was struck by lightning.
4. No change.
5. my neighbor's car; My neighbor's car was hit by the tree.
6. the car alarm; The car alarm was activated by the impact.
7. No change.
8. the roof of the car; The roof of the car was damaged by the tree.
9. No change.
10. my neighbor; My neighbor is going to be upset by the damage.

PRACTICE 13, p. 178
Checked sentences: 2, 4, 6, 9

PRACTICE 14, p. 178

	passive verb	action performed by
1.	are used	unknown
2.	was opened	Shelley
3.	will be translated	unknown
4.	was stolen	unknown
5.	was designed	a famous architect
6.	is going to be built	unknown
7.	has been rented	a young family with two small children
8.	has also been rented.	unknown

PRACTICE 15, p. 179
1. The soccer game has been canceled
2. The meeting has been canceled by the president.
3. Ethnic dishes are served at that restaurant.
4. I was confused in class yesterday.
5. I was confused by the teacher's directions.
6. The dishes haven't been washed yet.
7. They should be washed soon.
8. Was this sweater washed in hot water?
9. I was invited to the party by Luis.
10. Have you been invited to the party?

PRACTICE 16, p. 179
1. Sometimes keys are hidden under cars.
2. Cats hide under cars.
3. Students are taught by teachers.
4. Students study a lot.
5. Cereal is often eaten at breakfast.
6. Cats eat cat food.
7. Mice are eaten by cats.
8. Songs are sung to children by their mothers.
9. Thai food is cooked in Thai restaurants.
10. Chefs cook in restaurants.

PRACTICE 17, p. 180
1. b
2. b
3. a
4. b
5. b
6. a
7. b
8. a

PRACTICE 18, p. 180
1. I   It **happened** many years ago.
2. C   (No change.)
3. I   I **went** to school yesterday.
4. I   Two firefighters **were injured** while they were fighting the fire.
5. I   Sara **accidentally broke** the window.
6. C   (No change.)
7. I   Timmy was **eating** when the phone rang.
8. I   I **agree** with you.
9. I   The little boy **fell** down while he was running in the park.
10. I   The swimmer **died** from a shark attack.
11. C   (No change.)
12. I   I **slept** for nine hours last night.

PRACTICE 19, p. 181
1. has to be returned
2. should be returned
3. must be sent
4. could be sent
5. should be sent
6. can be put away
7. may be thrown away
8. might be picked up
9. will be cleaned up

PRACTICE 20, p. 182
1. a. The animal should be treated by a veterinarian.
   b. The animal will be given medicine.
2. a. No, the last paragraph has to be changed.
   b. No, it must be signed by Mr. Hayes.
3. a. It might be bought by a famous hockey star.
   b. It may be converted into apartments.
4. a. The credit card company should be called immediately.
   b. The mistake ought to be fixed right away.
5. a. It should be read by everyone.
   b. A movie of the book will be made.
6. a. It should be shortened.
   b. It has to be done soon.

PRACTICE 21, p. 182
1. were used . . . appeared . . . were made . . . were worn . . . began . . . were called . . . became . . . remained . . . were put . . . wore . . . have been manufactured
2. are being sold . . . is displayed . . . aren't needed . . . have never worn . . . may disappear . . . will be considered

PRACTICE 22, p. 183
Part I
1. to
2. about
3. from
4. of
5. in / with
6. of
7. with
8. in / with
9. about
10. with

Part II
11. in
12. with
13. of
14. to
15. to
16. with
17. from

Part III
18. of
19. in
20. with
21. for

PRACTICE 23, p. 183
1. The little girl is **excited about** her birthday party.
2. Mr. and Mrs. Rose **are devoted to** each other.
3. Could you please help me? I need directions. I **am** lost.
4. The students are **bored with** their chemistry project.
5. The paper bags at this store **are composed of** recycled products.
6. Your friend needs a doctor. He **is** hurt.
7. How well are you **prepared for** the driver's license test?
8. Mary has been **engaged to** Paul for five years. Will they ever get married?

PRACTICE 24, p. 184

1. interesting
2. interested
3. exciting
4. excited
5. fascinated
6. fascinating
7. boring . . . confusing
8. bored . . . confused
9. interesting
10. fascinating . . . surprising

PRACTICE 25, p. 184

1. interested
2. confusing . . . confused
3. excited . . . exciting
4. surprising . . . surprised
5. embarrassing . . . embarrassed
6. fascinating . . . fascinated
7. satisfying . . . satisfying
8. inspiring . . . inspired

PRACTICE 26, p. 185

1. confusing
2. frustrated
3. confusing
4. embarrassed
5. embarrassing
6. interested
7. interesting
8. exhausting . . . tired
9. frightening
10. frightened

PRACTICE 27, p. 185

1. c
2. a
3. b
4. a
5. c

PRACTICE 28, p. 186

1. g
2. c
3. a
4. h
5. b
6. f
7. d
8. e

PRACTICE 29, p. 186

1. Get
2. got
3. am getting
4. got
5. Get
6. get
7. got
8. get
9. am getting
10. am getting

PRACTICE 30, p. 187

1. b, c
2. a
3. b, c
4. a
5. a
6. b, c
7. b, c
8. a

PRACTICE 31, p. 187

1. Ø
2. is
3. are . . . am
4. Ø
5. is
6. Ø
7. Ø
8. is
9. is
10. Ø

PRACTICE 32, p. 188

1. used to get
2. is used to working
3. used to play
4. used to be
5. is used to working
6. is used to eating

PRACTICE 33, p. 188

1. I was supposed to return this book to the library.
2. We are supposed to read Chapter 9 before class tomorrow.
3. I was supposed to go to a party last night, but I stayed home.
4. We are supposed to do Exercise 10 for homework.
5. It is supposed to rain tomorrow.
6. I am / you are supposed to take one pill every six hours.
7. I am supposed to dust the furniture and vacuum the carpet.

PRACTICE 34, p. 189

1. The moving boxes **were** packed by Pierre.
2. My uncle **died** in the war.
3. Miami **is** located in Florida.
4. I was very wor**ried** about my son.
5. Mr. Rivera **is** interested in finding a new career.
6. Did you tell everyone the **shocking** news?
7. After ten years, I **am** finally used to this wet and rainy climate.
8. The newspaper **is supposed** to come every morning before eight.
9. The Millers have been mar**ried to** each other for 60 years.
10. I **used** to drink coffee with cream, but now I drink it black.
11. What happen**ed** at the party last night?
12. Several people almost **got killed** when the fireworks exploded over them.
13. A new parking garage **is** being **built** for our office.
14. I have been living in England for several years, so I **am accustomed to** driving on the left side of the road.

PRACTICE 35, p. 190

CHAPTER 11: COUNT/NONCOUNT NOUNS AND ARTICLES

PRACTICE 1, p. 191

1. a	9. an	16. a
2. an	10. an	17. an
3. a	11. an	18. a
4. an	12. a	19. an
5. a	13. a	20. a
6. a	14. an	21. a
7. an	15. a	22. an
8. a		

PRACTICE 2, p. 191

1. a chair	6. Some
2. chairs	7. Furniture
3. chairs	8. some
4. chair	9. desk
5. furniture	10. desks

PRACTICE 3, p. 192

Mail	Fruit	Jewelry	Furniture
bills	apples	bracelets	beds
checks	bananas	earrings	chairs
letters	oranges	necklaces	sofas
packages	strawberries	rings	tables

PRACTICE 4, p. 192

1. water	4. gold
2. light	5. help
3. thunder	6. fun

PRACTICE 5, p. 192

1. Ø . . . Ø
2. Ø . . . boots . . . socks
3. cookies . . . Ø
4. Ø . . . Ø . . . Ø
5. Ø . . . bones
6. Ø . . . Ø
7. Ø . . . Ø

PRACTICE 6, p. 193

1. word	words
2. Ø	vocabulary
3. Ø	slang
4. Ø	homework
5. assignment	assignments
6. dress	dresses
7. Ø	clothing
8. family	families
9. Ø	knowledge
10. Ø	information
11. fact	facts
12. Ø	luck

PRACTICE 7, p. 193

1. Tom lived in a big city for many years. However, three years ago he left the city. It had Ø pollution and Ø smog, and he couldn't breathe well. Now he lives in a small town in the mountains. He breathes Ø clean air and drinks Ø fresh water. He knows that it was a good idea to leave the city because his health is better.

2. Cornell University is named for Ezra Cornell. Ezra Cornell was a philanthropist who lived in Ithaca, New York. He loved the area and wanted to improve it. People there didn't have a library, and so he built one for them. Then, he wanted to build a university where people could gain Ø knowledge in Ø practical subjects, such as farming, as well as in Ø history, Ø literature, and Ø science. Cornell owned a large farm in the area, and in an act of generosity, he donated it as the site for the new university. Cornell University opened in 1865, and today it is known as an excellent university — one of the best universities in the world.

PRACTICE 8, p. 194

1. bread, corn, peas, and rice.
2. apple trees, grass, lakes, mountains, and scenery.
3. bracelets, jewels, jewelry, and rings.
4. equipment, machines, machinery, and tools.

PRACTICE 9, p. 194

1. one		9. one
2. much		10. much
3. many		11. many
4. much		12. much
5. much		13. much
6. much		14. one
7. much		15. many
8. many		16. many

PRACTICE 10, p. 194

1. a. apples, vegetables
   b. coffee, fruit, sugar
2. a. answers, persons (OR people), things
   b. English, slang
3. a. ideas, suggestions
   b. homework, information, work
4. a. police officers
   b. crime, garbage, traffic, violence

PRACTICE 11, p. 195

1. many letters are
2. much mail Ø
3. many men have
4. much English literature Ø
5. many English words
6. much gasoline Ø
7. much petrol Ø
8. many grandchildren
9. much fun Ø
10. many islands are
11. many people Ø
12. many zeroes / zeros are

PRACTICE 12, p. 195

1. a	11. a
2. some, many	12. an
3. a	13. some, many
4. some, much	14. some, much
5. some, many	15. a
6. some, much	16. some, much
7. an	17. a
8. a	18. an
9. an	19. some, much
10. some, many	20. some, many

PRACTICE 13, p. 196

1. a little . . . Ø
2. a little . . . Ø
3. a few oranges
4. a little . . . Ø
5. a little . . . Ø
6. a few suggestions
7. a few questions
8. a few . . . Ø
9. a few . . . minutes
10. a little . . . Ø
11. a little . . . Ø
12. a little . . . Ø

PRACTICE 14, p. 196

1. d, f, g, h   5. a, c, f, h
2. c, e   6. d, g
3. c, d
4. c

PRACTICE 15, p. 197

(1) Scientists . . . animals . . . plants . . . place
(2) flowers . . . trees . . . deserts . . . oceans . . . mountains
(3) Rice . . . crop . . . world . . . crops . . . weather . . . fields
(4) Plants . . . health . . . air . . . trees . . . earth . . . air

PRACTICE 16, p. 198

1. e   6. h
2. a   7. b
3. g   8. f
4. i   9. c
5. j   10. d

PRACTICE 17, p. 198

1. jar   6. bag / box
2. bottle   7. jar
3. box   8. bottle
4. jar   9. bag / box
5. can / tin   10. can / tin

PRACTICE 18, p. 198

1. cup
2. pounds / kilos
3. glass
4. gallons
5. bottle / carton
6. piece
7. pieces
8. piece
9. sheets / pieces
10. loaf
11. piece
12. piece

PRACTICE 19, p. 199

1. many suitcases
2. much sunscreen
3. many pairs of sandals
4. much toothpaste
5. much luggage
6. much money
7. many days

PRACTICE 20, p. 199

1. a   9. some
2. some   10. an
3. some   11. some
4. a   12. a
5. some   13. some
6. an   14. a
7. some   15. some
8. a

PRACTICE 21, p. 200

1. a . . . some . . . a . . . some . . . some
2. some . . . some . . . some . . . some
3. some . . . some . . . a . . . a . . . some

PRACTICE 22, p. 200

1. A
2. the
3. a . . . a . . . a
4. the . . . the
5. the
6. a
7. a . . . a
8. the . . . the
9. a
10. the
11. a . . . a
12. The . . . the . . . the
13. a
14. the

PRACTICE 23, p. 201

1. some . . . a . . . The . . . the
2. some . . . a . . . a . . . a . . . The . . . The . . . the
3. A: an
   A: A . . . a . . . a
   B: the
   A: The . . . the . . . the
4. a . . . a . . . an . . . The . . . the . . . the . . . the . . . the

PRACTICE 24, p. 201

1. a   11. a
2. a   12. the
3. a   13. the
4. The   14. the
5. a   15. the
6. the   16. a
7. the   17. the
8. the   18. the
9. the   19. the
10. the

PRACTICE 25, p. 202

1. a . . . Ø . . . Ø
2. Ø
3. The
4. The . . . a . . . the . . . Ø . . . Ø . . . Ø
5. A: the
   B: the
6. the . . . the
7. Ø . . . Ø . . . Ø
8. A: the
   B: the . . . the
9. an . . . A . . . a . . . a . . . Ø . . . the . . . the . . . the

PRACTICE 26, p. 203

1. Ø
2. Ø
3. Ø . . . the
4. The . . . Ø
5. Ø . . . Ø
6. Ø . . . Ø
7. Ø
8. The . . . Ø . . . Ø
9. Ø
10. Ø . . . Ø . . . Ø
11. The
12. The . . . Ø . . . The . . . the

PRACTICE 27, p. 204

1. **the** Dead Sea
2. **the** Amazon River
3. Shanghai
4. **the** Sahara Desert
5. **the** Thames River
6. Europe
7. **the** Alps
8. Lake Tanganyika
9. North America
10. **the** Indian Ocean
11. **the** Netherlands
12. North America
13. Nepal
14. **the** Urals
15. Lagos
16. **the** United Arab Emirates

PRACTICE 28, p. 204

1. I'm taking **B**iology 101 this semester.
2. I'm taking history, biology, **E**nglish, and calculus this semester.
3. Some lab classes meet on **S**aturday.
4. My roommate likes **V**ietnamese food, and **I** like **T**hai food.
5. Shelia works for the **X**erox corporation. **I**t is a very large corporation.
6. Pedro is from **L**atin **A**merica. He speaks **S**panish.
7. My favorite park is **C**entral **P**ark in **N**ew **Y**ork.
8. No change.
9. I like **U**ncle **J**oe and **A**unt **S**ara.
10. **S**usan **W**. **M**iller is a professor.
11. I am in **P**rof. **M**iller's class.
12. In **J**anuary, it's winter in **C**anada and summer in **A**rgentina.
13. I would like to visit **L**os **A**ngeles.
14. It's the largest city in **C**alifornia.

PRACTICE 29, p. 205

Correct the errors.

1. The mail carrier brought only one **letter** today.
2. Mr. Dale gave his class **a** long history assignment for the weekend.
3. Tariq speaks several languages, including Arabic and German.
4. I usually have **a** glass **of** water with my lunch.
5. A helpful police officer gave us (**some**) **information** about the city.
6. This recipe calls for two cups **of** nut**s**.
7. **Many** vegetable**s** are believed to have cancer-fighting ingredients.

8. Only applicants with the necessary **experience** should apply for the computer position.
9. When Vicki likes a movie, she sees it several time**s**.
10. No change.
11. Is it possible to stop all **violence** in the world?
12. Some of the **homework** for my English class was easy, but many of the assignment**s** were unclear.
13. Diane has been to Rome several time**s** recently. She always has **a** wonderful time.
14. Many parents need **advice** about raising children.
15. A person doesn't need **much** equipment to play baseball: just **a** ball and a bat.

PRACTICE 30, p. 206

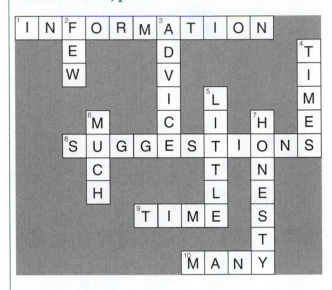

CHAPTER 12: ADJECTIVE CLAUSES

PRACTICE 1, p. 207

1. who helped me move the refrigerator
   1: I thanked
   2: He helped
2. who was wearing a gray suit
   1: A woman asked
   2: She was wearing
3. that was wearing a blue coat
   1: I saw
   2: He was wearing
4. who had pulled his brother from the icy river
   1: The parents hugged
   2: He had pulled
5. that broke the vase
   1: The girl apologized
   2: She broke

PRACTICE 2, p. 208

Adjective clauses:
    S V
1. who live next to me
    S V
2. who live across the street
    S V
3. that is from India
    S V
4. who have children

S   V
5. who teaches at the university
S   V
6. who is training to play basketball in the Special Olympics.

PRACTICE 3, p. 208
1. *Long sentence 1*:   The woman who answered the phone was polite.

   Long sentence 2:   The woman that answered the phone was polite.
2. *Long sentence 1*:   The man who played the guitar is also a singer.

   Long sentence 2:   The man that played the guitar is also a singer.
3. *Long sentence 1*:   I read about the soccer player who was injured yesterday.

   Long sentence 2:   I read about the soccer player that was injured yesterday.
4. *Long sentence 1*:   I know a man who has sailed around the world.

   Long sentence 2:   I know a man that has sailed around the world.

PRACTICE 4, p. 209
1. who / that cuts hair
2. who / that makes pizza
3. who / that plays tennis
4. who / that teaches English
5. who / that trains horses
6. who / that eats meat
7. who / that drink tea
8. who / that fight fires

PRACTICE 5, p. 209
1. The woman that Jack met was polite.
2. The woman Jack saw was very tall.
3. The woman that Jack knows is a professor.
4. The student that the teacher helped was thankful.
5. The student I helped was happy about the exam.
6. The student who I just met won a scholarship.
7. The student whom you see over there is the class president.

PRACTICE 6, p. 210
1. S   7. O who
2. O that   8. O who
3. S   9. S
4. O that   10. O that
5. S   11. S
6. S

PRACTICE 7, p. 210
1. a, b, c, d   4. c, d
2. c, d   5. b, d
3. a, b, c, d   6. a, b, c

PRACTICE 8, p. 211
1. who / that
2. that / Ø / who / whom
3. that / Ø / who / whom
4. who / that
5. who / that
6. that / Ø / who / whom

PRACTICE 9, p. 211
1. b   5. a
2. a   6. a
3. b   7. b
4. b   8. b

PRACTICE 10, p. 212
1. O which   5. S
2. S   6. S
3. O that   7. S
4. O which   8. O that

PRACTICE 11, p. 212
1. that / which / Ø   4. that / which / Ø
2. that / which   5. that / which
3. that / which / Ø

PRACTICE 12, p. 213
1. I visited
2. that I drank
3. I was wearing
4. that I've known and loved
5. who I married
6. that we have had
7. which we bought

PRACTICE 13, p. 213
1. a, b, d, e   6. c, d, e
2. a, d   7. a, b, d, e
3. c, d   8. c, d, e
4. c, d, e   9. a, d
5. a, d   10. c, d

PRACTICE 14, p. 214
1. students . . . are   6. student . . . is
2. people . . . are   7. people . . . live
3. compound . . . consists 8. person . . . makes
4. students . . . speak   9. artists . . . make
5. people . . . know

PRACTICE 15, p. 215
1. a. we went to
   b. we went to
2. a. you introduced me to
   b. you introduced me to
3. a. I am quite familiar with
   b. which I am quite familiar
4. a. you should talk with
   b. whom you should talk
5. a. we are waiting for
   b. we are waiting for
6. a. I'm interested in
   b. I'm interested in

PRACTICE 16, p. 215
1. a. that . . . for   3. a. that . . . in
   b. which . . . for   b. which . . . in
   c. Ø . . . for   c. Ø . . . in
   d. which . . . Ø   d. which . . . Ø
2. a. that . . . to   4. a. that . . . with
   b. which . . . to   b. Ø . . . with
   c. Ø . . . to   c. who . . . with
   d. which . . . Ø   d. that . . . with
                              e. whom . . . Ø

PRACTICE 17, p. 216

1. I enjoyed the CD [we listened **to** at Sara's apartment.]
2. I paid the shopkeeper for the glass cup [I accidentally broke Ø.]
3. The bus [we were waiting **for**] was only three minutes late.
4. Mrs. Chan is someone [I always enjoy talking **to** about politics.]
5. I showed my roommate the letter [I got from a co-worker Ø.]
6. One of the subjects [I've been interested **in** for a long time] is astronomy.
7. The people [I talked **to** at the reception] were interesting.
8. One of the places [I want to visit Ø next year] is Mexico City.
9. The website [I was looking **at**] had useful reviews of new computers.
10. The book [I wanted Ø] wasn't available at the library.
11. English grammar is one of the subjects [Ø which I enjoy studying the most.]
12. The friend [I waved **to** / **at**] didn't wave back. Maybe he just didn't see me.

PRACTICE 18, p. 216

1. whose daughter is a test-pilot
   1: I know a man.
   2: His daughter is a test-pilot.
2. whose husband is out of work
   1: The woman found a job at Mel's Diner.
   2: Her husband is out of work.
3. whose wallet I found
   1: The man gave me a reward.
   2: I found his wallet.

PRACTICE 19, p. 217

1. The firefighters are very brave. Their department has won many awards.
   → The firefighters whose department has won many awards are very brave.
2. I talked to the boy. His kite was caught in a tree.
   → I talked to the boy whose kite was caught in a tree.
3. The family is staying in a motel. Their house burned down.
   → The family whose house burned down is staying in a motel.
4. I watched a little girl. Her dog was chasing a ball in the park.
   → I watched a little girl whose dog was chasing a ball in the park.
5. The reporter won an award. Her articles explained global warming.
   → The reporter whose articles explained global warming won an award.
6. I know a man. His daughter entered college at the age of 14.
   → I know a man whose daughter entered college at the age of 14.
7. We observed a language teacher. Her teaching methods included role-playing.
   → We observed a language teacher whose teaching methods included role-playing.

8. The teachers are very popular. Their methods include role-playing.
   → The teachers whose methods include role-playing are very popular.

PRACTICE 20, p. 217

True (checked) answers:

1. a, c
2. c
3. b, c
4. c
5. a
6. a, c

PRACTICE 21, p. 218

1. who / that
2. who / that
3. that / which / Ø
4. whose
5. that / which
6. Ø / that / who / whom
7. whose
8. that / which
9. who / that
10. Ø / that / who / whom
11. who / that . . . Ø / that / who / whom . . . whom

PRACTICE 22, p. 218

1. a
2. b
3. b
4. b
5. a
6. a
7. a
8. b

PRACTICE 23, p. 219

1. A movie that **looks** interesting opens tomorrow.
2. My family lived in a house **that** / **which was** built in 1900.
3. There's the man that we **saw** on TV.
4. I don't know people **whose** lives are carefree.
5. It is important to help people who **have** no money.
6. At the airport, I was waiting for friends Ø / **that** / **who** / **whom** I hadn't **seen** for a long time.
7. The woman **who** / **that** lives next door likes to relax by doing crossword puzzles every evening.
8. My teacher has two cats **whose** names are Ping and Pong.
9. I enjoyed the songs which we **sang**.
10. The person to **whom** you should speak is Gary Green.

PRACTICE 24, p. 220

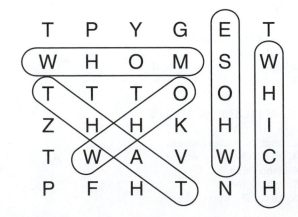

CHAPTER 13: GERUNDS AND INFINITIVES

PRACTICE 1, p. 221
1. moving
2. living
3. taking
4. buying
5. giving
6. doing
7. reviewing
8. finding
9. driving
10. retiring
11. getting married
12. working

PRACTICE 2, p. 221
1. went dancing
2. is going to go hiking
3. went shopping
4. go swimming
5. goes fishing
6. go sightseeing
7. go camping
8. go sailing
9. go skiing
10. went skydiving

PRACTICE 3, p. 222
1. to wait   INF
2. walking   GER
3. to help   INF
4. cleaning   GER
5. to order   INF
6. quitting   GER
7. to work   INF
8. to grow   INF

PRACTICE 4, p. 222
1. to invite
2. being
3. to pay
4. mailing
5. to pass
6. to consider
7. accepting
8. reading
9. visiting
10. to hurt
11. asking
12. to look
13. to try
14. to enjoy
15. opening
16. to keep
17. to give
18. to support
19. to finish

PRACTICE 5, p. 223
1. b
2. a, b
3. a, b
4. b
5. a, b
6. a, b
7. a, b
8. b
9. a
10. a, b
11. a, b
12. a, b
13. b
14. a
15. b

PRACTICE 6, p. 224
1. to go . . . to pay . . . to get . . . to apply . . . to receive
2. to take . . to go . . . to go . . . being . . . to go . . . skiing . . . swimming . . . sailing
3. getting . . . to tell . . . leaving . . . to have . . . to create . . . to take

PRACTICE 7, p. 224
Part I
1. to work
2. working
3. to work
4. working
5. to work
6. to work / working
7. to work
8. to work
9. working
10. to work
11. to work
12. working
Part II
13. to leave
14. to leave
15. leaving
16. leaving
17. leaving
18. leaving
19. to leave
20. to leave
21. leaving
22. to leave
Part III
23. to know
24. to know
25. to know
26. knowing
27. to know
28. to know
29. to know / knowing
30. to know
31. to know
32. to know / knowing

PRACTICE 8, p. 225
Part I
1. of flying
2. for hurting
3. in helping
4. at listening
5. of working
6. about walking
7. of / about owning
8. about buying
Part II
9. for closing
10. for lending
11. on becoming
12. for taking
13. on eating
14. to finishing
15. from making
16. about . . . having

PRACTICE 9, p. 226
1. for . . . for interrupting
2. in . . . in learning
3. for . . . for helping
4. on . . . on walking
5. for . . . for losing
6. like . . . like going
7. at . . . at drawing
8. in . . . in saving
9. about . . . about forgetting
10. about . . . about going
11. to . . . to going
12. of . . . of staying

PRACTICE 10, p. 226
Part I
1. e
2. f
3. a
4. b
5. c
6. d

Part II

7. j
8. k
9. l
10. g
11. h
12. i

PRACTICE 11, p. 227
(1) doing . . . doing / to do . . . to do
(2) to write . . . doing . . . thinking
(3) for being . . . to thank . . . sending . . . wearing . . . to wear
(4) to seeing . . . for taking

PRACTICE 12, p. 228
1. going
2. of driving
3. watching
4. cooking / to cook
5. of going
6. about becoming
7. having
8. running
9. on washing
10. from hitting
11. to be
12. about seeing

PRACTICE 13, p. 228
1. by holding
2. by reading
3. by telling
4. by watching
5. by running
6. by treating

PRACTICE 14, p. 229
1. by taking
2. by pouring
3. by stretching
4. by working
5. by saving
6. by following
7. by looking
8. by counting

PRACTICE 15, p. 230
1. a, d, e, f
2. a, b, c
3. b, c, d, f
4. a, b, d, e, f

PRACTICE 16, p. 230
1. a. It is . . . to learn
   b. Learning . . . is
2. a. Eating . . . is
   b. It is . . . to eat
3. a. Driving . . . is
   b. It is . . . to drive
4. a. It is . . . to swim
   b. Swimming . . . is
5. a. Is it . . . to live
   b. Is living
6. a. Is it . . . to complete
   b. Is completing

PRACTICE 17, p. 231
1. It is difficult for shy people to meet . . .
2. it is customary for young children to sleep . . .
3. It is necessary for airline pilots to have . . .
4. It is hard for many teenagers to wake up . . .
5. It is important for elderly people to keep . . .
6. It is boring for people to listen . . .
7. It is impossible for scientists to know . . .

PRACTICE 18, p. 231
1. a. for
   b. to
   c. to
   d. for
   e. to
   f. to
   g. for
2. a. to
   b. for
   c. for
   d. to
   e. to
   f. for
   g. to

PRACTICE 19, p. 231
1. to
2. for
3. for
4. to
5. for
6. to
7. to
8. for
9. to
10. for
11. for

PRACTICE 20, p. 232
1. turned on the TV (in order) to watch the news.
2. goes to the laundromat (in order) to wash his clothes.
3. runs (in order) to get to class on time.
4. open the bedroom windows (in order) to let in some fresh air.
5. calls his parents (in order) to ask them for some money.
6. have the radio on (in order) to listen to a baseball game.
7. go to the library (in order) to study in peace and quiet.

PRACTICE 21, p. 232
1. a. enough time to go
   b. too busy to go
2. a. tall enough
   b. too short
3. a. enough money
   b. too poor
4. a. too hot
   b. cool enough
5. a. too sick
   b. well enough
6. a. isn't old enough
   b. is too young

PRACTICE 22, p. 233
1. Ø . . . enough
2. too . . . Ø
3. Ø . . . enough
4. too . . . Ø
5. too . . . Ø
6. Ø . . . enough
7. too . . . Ø
8. Ø . . . enough

PRACTICE 23, p. 233
1. being
2. to spend
3. being
4. being
5. to find
6. being
7. to talk / talking
8. sitting
9. thinking
10. to think
11. speaking
12. making
13. to discuss

PRACTICE 24, p. 234

1. Studying
2. writing
3. to be
4. B: flying
   A: crashing
5. A: arguing . . . to disagree
   B: raising . . . to yell
   A: to get
6. A: to have
   B: to learn
7. A: doing
   B: going shopping
   A: shopping
8. A: putting
   B: forgetting to send

PRACTICE 25, p. 235

1. I decided not **to buy** a new car.
2. The Johnsons are considering **selling** their antique store.
3. Sam finally finished **building** his vacation home in the mountains.
4. My wife and I **go dancing** at the community center every Saturday night.
5. Suddenly, it began to **rain** and the wind started to **blow**.
6. The baby is afraid **of being** away from her mother for any length of time.
7. I am excited **about starting** college this September.
8. You can send your application **by** fax.
9. My country is **very** beautiful.
10. **It is** exciting to drive a sports car.
11. My grandparents enjoy **traveling** across the country in a motor home.
12. Elena made this sweater **by hand**.
13. Running **is** one of the sports we can participate in at school.
14. **Swimming** with a group of people is more enjoyable than **swimming** alone.
15. Meeting new people **is** interesting.

PRACTICE 26, p. 236

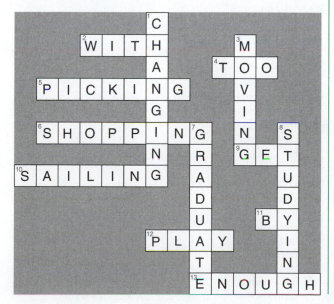

CHAPTER 14: NOUN CLAUSES

PRACTICE 1, p. 237

1. . noun clause
2. ? question
3. . noun clause
4. ? question
5. ? question
6. . noun clause
7. ? question
8. . noun clause
9. . noun clause
10. ? question
11. ? question
12. . noun clause

PRACTICE 2, p. 237

1. Helen works
2. Adam said
3. we are doing this
4. the new semester starts
5. everyone went
6. people believe
7. believes that story
8. cell phone is ringing

PRACTICE 3, p. 238

1. Vince lives
2. that woman is
3. Henri did
4. her phone number is
5. keys these are
6. Clara met
7. Carlo is absent
8. it is
9. Sam is studying
10. called
11. Ms. Gray will call
12. the president is going to say
13. is in that room
14. is in that drawer
15. a GPS system costs

PRACTICE 4, p. 238

1. did Marcos leave? . . . when Marcos left?
2. did he say? . . . what he said.
3. is the post office? . . . where the post office is?
4. is it? . . . what time it is?
5. did David arrive? . . . when David arrived.
6. is Ana from? . . . what country Ana is from.
7. was Kathy . . . why Kathy was . . .
8. lives . . . who lives . . .
9. car is . . . whose car is . . .
10. books are these? . . . whose books these are?

PRACTICE 5, p. 239

1. who Helen talked to
2. who lives
3. what he said
4. what kind of car Pat has
5. how old their children are
6. why you said
7. where I can catch
8. what this word means

PRACTICE 6, p. 240

1. b
2. a
3. a
4. b
5. b
6. a
7. b
8. a
9. a
10. b
11. a
12. b

PRACTICE 7, p. 240
1. people are saying . . . all the buildings are . . . my classes start . . . I register . . . I am taking . . . my professors will be
2. it will take . . . I came . . . I am

PRACTICE 8, p. 241
1. if / whether Tom is coming
2. if / whether Jin has finished medical school yet
3. if / whether Daniel has any time off soon
4. if / whether the flight is on time
5. if / whether there is enough gas in the car
6. if / whether Yuki is married
7. if / whether the Nelsons are going to move
8. if / whether Khaled changed jobs

PRACTICE 9, p. 241
1. if I'm going to need
2. what you want
3. if there is going to be
4. where birds go
5. if you can borrow
6. if Nasser has already left
7. why Harold left

PRACTICE 10, p. 242
1. rains
2. gets
3. like
4. runs
5. run
6. takes
7. enjoy
8. seems

PRACTICE 11, p. 242
1. c
2. f
3. a
4. g
5. h
6. b
7. d
8. e

PRACTICE 12, p. 243
1. I'm sorry that . . .
2. I predict that . . .
3. I'm surprised that . . .
4. Are you certain that . . .
5. Did you notice that . . .
6. It's a fact that . . .
7. A: How do you know that . . .
   A: I'm still worried that . . .
8: A: I heard that . . .
   A: Some people assume that. . . I think that . . .

PRACTICE 13, p. 243
1. are pleased that their granddaughter graduated from the university
   are glad that she was offered a good job
2. were worried that Po had been injured
   they were happy when Po called
3. was afraid that he had failed
   was not surprised that he had done well
4. was angry that Mark lied to her
   is sorry that she lent him money
5. that exercise can be good for the heart
   that eating a lot of red meat is bad for the heart

PRACTICE 14, p. 244
1. that Alice has a car
2. that the library is open on Sunday
3. that Ann speaks Spanish
4. that Alex passed his French course
5. that Mr. Kozari is going to be at the meeting
6. that these pants are clean

PRACTICE 15, p. 244
1. Alex asked, "**D**o you smell smoke**?**"
2. "**S**omething is burning," he said.
3. He asked, "**D**o you smell smoke**? S**omething is burning."
4. "**D**o you smell smoke**?**" he asked. "**S**omething is burning."
5. **R**achel said,"**T**he game starts at seven."
6. "**T**he game starts at seven. **W**e should leave here at six," she said.
7. She said, "**T**he game starts at seven. **W**e should leave here at six. **C**an you be ready to leave then**?**"

PRACTICE 16, p. 245
One day my friend Laura and I were sitting in her apartment. We were having a cup of tea together and talking about the terrible earthquake that had just occurred in Iran. Laura asked me, "Have you ever been in an earthquake?"

"Yes, I have," I replied.

"Was it a big earthquake?" she asked.

"I've been in several earthquakes, and they've all been small ones," I answered. "Have you ever been in an earthquake?"

"There was an earthquake in my village five years ago," Laura said. "I was in my house. Suddenly the ground started shaking. I grabbed my little brother and ran outside. Everything was moving. I was scared to death. And then suddenly it was over."

"I'm glad you and your brother weren't hurt," I said.

"Yes, we were very lucky. Has everyone in the world felt an earthquake sometime in their lives?" Laura wondered. "Do earthquakes occur everywhere on the earth?"

"Those are interesting questions," I said, "but I don't know the answers."

PRACTICE 17, p. 246
1. he . . . his
2. his . . . them
3. she . . . her
4. him . . . them
5. they . . . me . . . they
6. she . . . her
7. they . . . my
8. he . . . us . . . they . . . his

PRACTICE 18, p. 246

	Formal	Informal
1.	would meet	will meet
2.	was going to be	is going to be
3.	had	has
4.	needed	needs
5.	had flown	has flown
6.	were planning	are planning
7.	didn't want	doesn't want
8.	could take care of	can take care of

PRACTICE 19, p. 247

1. (that) you didn't have
2. (that) you hadn't found
3. (that) the Smiths had canceled
4. (that) it wouldn't rain
5. (that) the Whites had gotten
6. (that) Mei didn't exercise
7. (that) your computer wasn't working
8. (that) Ali was coming

PRACTICE 20, p. 248

1. how old I was
2. if he was going to be
3. if she had
4. if he had changed his
5. how long I had been
6. if she could speak
7. if he would be in his office
8. why she was laughing
9. if I had ever considered

PRACTICE 21, p. 248

1. "Have you ever gone skydiving?"
2. "Will you be at the meeting?"
3. "Are you going to quit your job?"
4. "Where is your car?"
5. "What did you do after class yesterday?"
6. "Do you know Italian?"
7. "Can you pick up my daughter at school?"
8. "Why aren't you working at your desk?"

PRACTICE 22, p. 249

1. why I had come here
2. if I had met many people
3. what I was going to study
4. how long I would stay
5. how I liked it here
6. where I was from
7. if the local people were friendly to me
8. how I had chosen this school
9. if I liked the weather here

PRACTICE 23, p. 249

1. (that) he was going to call me
2. (that) he had to talk to her
3. (that) she could meet me
4. (that) she wrote / had written him
5. she would see him
6. what he was doing

PRACTICE 24, p. 250

1. told
2. said
3. asked
4. told
5. said
6. told . . . said
7. asked . . . told . . . said
8. told . . . told
9. told
10. asked . . . said . . . asked . . . told

PRACTICE 25, p. 251

1. asked me where I lived.
2. asked me if / whether I lived
3. told him / replied / said that I had
4. told me / said that he was looking
5. told me / said that he didn't like living
6. asked him if / whether he wanted to move in with me.
7. asked me where my apartment was.
8. replied / told him / said that I lived
9. told me / said that he couldn't move
10. told me / said that he would cancel his
11. asked me if / whether that was okay.
12. told him / replied / said that I was looking forward to having him

PRACTICE 26, p. 251

1. b, e
2. a, b, c, d
3. b, f
4. a, d
5. a, c, e

PRACTICE 27, p. 252

1. that it was a beautiful day and he loved playing in the sun
2. what he was doing . . . where he was going
3. that he was carrying food to the nest
4. why he was working so hard in the beautiful summer weather
5. that if he brought food to the nest in the summer, he could have food in the winter
6. if he could take a break then, and play with him instead of working
7. that he couldn't
8. that if he didn't bring food to the nests in the summer, he wouldn't have any food for the winter
9. that he wasn't worried about the winter because he had plenty of food
10. if those ants ever had any fun
11. that the ants were smart because they had prepared for the winter
12. that it was always a good idea to prepare for the future

PRACTICE 28, p. 253

1. Excuse me. May I ask how old **you are**?
2. I wonder **if** Rashed **picked** up something for dinner.
3. I'm unsure what Lawrence **does** for a living.
4. Fernando said, **"T**he best time for me to meet would be Thursday morning.**"**
5. Eriko **asked** me **if I was** coming to the graduation party. I **told** her that I wasn't.
6. I **hope that** I will do well on my final exams.
7. I'm not sure **if the** price includes the sales tax or not.
8. My mother **asked me**, "How many hours did you spend on your homework?"
9. I **asked** my brother, "Are **you** going to marry Paula?"
10. I'd like to know **how you** do that.
11. My parents knew what Sam and I **did.**
12. **It is** a fact that unexpected things happen in everyone's lives.

PRACTICE 29, p. 254

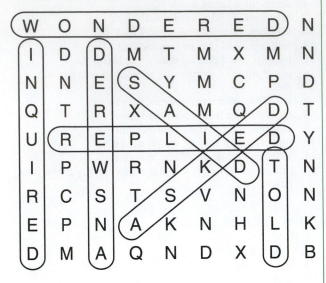

APPENDIX 1: PHRASAL VERBS

PRACTICE 2, p. 255
1. off . . . on
2. up
3. up . . . down
4. off . . . in
5. down . . . up
6. up
7. up . . . off
8. away
9. out . . . out

PRACTICE 3, p. 256
1. the TV, the stove
2. my coat, my wedding ring
3. his shoes
4. a story, a fairy tale, an excuse
5. some rotten food, an old shirt
6. a doctor's appointment, a meeting, a trip
7. a puzzle, a math problem
8. a report, some late homework
9. a message, a phone number
10. a box, a sack of mail
11. the light, the computer, the car engine

PRACTICE 5, p. 257
1. on
2. over
3. on . . . off
4. into / in . . . out of
5. on . . . off
6. into
7. into

PRACTICE 6, p. 257
1. b   5. f
2. c   6. d
3. a   7. e
4. g

PRACTICE 8, p. 258
1. back
2. down
3. out
4. away
5. on
6. up
7. back
8. up
9. back
10. off
11. out . . . up . . . off . . . back

PRACTICE 9, p. 259
1. out . . . out   7. down . . . X
2. on . . . X   8. X . . . up
3. into . . . X   9. away . . . X
4. X . . . into   10. up . . . up
5. up . . . up   11. off . . . X
6. away . . . away   12. from . . . X

PRACTICE 11, p. 260
1. over   8. out of
2. out   9. up
3. in   10. out
4. out   11. out
5. out   12. up
6. down   13. over
7. around

PRACTICE 12, p. 261
1. a. off   5. a. into
   b. on   b. up
   c. down   c. over
   d. back   6. a. up
   e. out   b. off
   f. away   c. back
2. a. in   7. a. off
   b. out   b. back
3. a. over   c. up
   b. off   d. over
   c. on   8. a. in
   d. into   b. out
   e. out of   c. up
4. a. up   d. up
   b. up
   c. down

PRACTICE 14, p. 263
1. on   9. up
2. up   10. on
3. out   11. up
4. over   12. over
5. out   13. up
6. away . . . out 14. away
7. out . . . up   15. out
8. off   16. away

PRACTICE 16, p. 264
1. off   7. out
2. up   8. back
3. over   9. up
4. down   10. up
5. down   11. on
6. up   12. in . . . down

PRACTICE 17, p. 265

1.		2.		3.	
a.	up	a.	up	a.	out of . . . into
b.	up	b.	up	b.	out
c.	up	c.	up	c.	up
d.	out	d.	up		
e.	out	e.	into		
f.	out of	f.	up		

PRACTICE 19, p. 266

1. out . . . out for
2. up
3. up for
4. out of
5. around with
6. back from
7. out of
8. out for
9. through with
10. in on
11. along with

PRACTICE 20, p. 267

1. gymnastics class
2. their neighbors
3. paint
4. rocks
5. assignment
6. cord
7. Hawaii
8. snakes

PRACTICE 22, p. 268

1. out . . . about
2. out for
3. back to
4. out with
5. away from
6. along with
7. over to
8. out of
9. A: over to
   B: around . . . with

PRACTICE 23, p. 268

1. out about
2. out
3. back
4. together
5. up to

PRACTICE 24, p. 268

1. a
2. b
3. a
4. c
5. a
6. b
7. d
8. b
9. c
10. d
11. b
12. d
13. a
14. c
15. a
16. d
17. c
18. a
19. a
20. d
21. b

APPENDIX 2: PREPOSITION COMBINATIONS

PRACTICE 2, p. 271

1. b
2. f
3. j
4. e
5. c
6. i
7. a
8. h
9. d
10. g

PRACTICE 3, p. 271

1. to
2. to
3. to
4. with
5. for
6. about
7. of
8. about
9. from
10. with
11. about
12. of

PRACTICE 5, p. 272

1. from
2. with
3. to
4. at
5. in
6. at
7. for
8. with . . . about / over
9. with
10. for
11. for

PRACTICE 6, p. 272

1. to
2. A: from
   B: for
3. A: to
   B: at
4. to
5. of
6. from . . . for
7. A: for . . . with
   B: to

PRACTICE 8, p. 273

1. to
2. for
3. for
4. of
5. for . . . for
6. for
7. to . . . from
8. to / with
9. about . . . in
10. of / about

PRACTICE 9, p. 274

1.		2.	
a.	of	a.	about
b.	for	b.	about
c.	of / about	c.	of
d.	with	d.	of
e.	with	e.	of
f.	of	f.	about
g.	in	g.	for
h.	to	h.	for

PRACTICE 11, p. 275

1. for
2. from
3. for
4. on
5. with
6. in
7. at
8. to
9. with
10. of
11. to
12. to . . . about
13. with . . . about
14. to . . . about

PRACTICE 12, p. 275

1. about
2. from
3. of
4. to
5. to
6. from
7. with
8. with
9. for . . . at
10. A: with . . . about
    B: to
    A: to . . . about

PRACTICE 14, p. 276

1. with
2. to
3. from
4. about
5. to
6. about / of
7. at
8. for
9. for
10. for
11. about
12. to
13. about / of
14. like
15. for
16. at

PRACTICE 15, p. 277

1. g
2. i
3. c
4. j
5. b
6. h
7. a
8. f
9. e
10. d

PRACTICE 17, p. 278

1. to . . . for
2. for
3. of
4. for
5. on
6. for
7. on
8. to / with
9. from
10. on
11. of
12. of
13. to
14. from
15. of / from

PRACTICE 18, p. 278

Correct sentences:

1. a, b
2. a
3. a, b
4. b
5. a, b
6. a, b
7. a
8. b

PRACTICE 20, p. 279

1. on
2. from
3. about
4. for
5. about
6. from
7. to / with . . . about
8. to
9. by
10. from
11. by
12. to
13. about
14. from

PRACTICE 21, p. 280

1. on
2. about
3. with
4. from
5. from
6. to . . . for
7. of
8. to
9. from
10. to
11. to
12. for
13. from
14. on
15. on
16. of
17. about

PRACTICE 22, p. 280

1. d
2. b
3. c
4. a
5. d
6. a
7. b
8. c
9. d
10. c
11. d
12. b
13. b
14. a
15. d
16. b
17. c
18. b
19. a
20. d
21. a
22. c

NOTES

NOTES

NOTES

NOTES

NOTES

NOTES

NOTES

NOTES